Beating the Boundaries

The Church God Is Calling Us to Be

Morehouse Publishing, 19 East 34th Street, New York, NY 10016
Morehouse Publishing is an imprint of Church Publishing Incorporated.
www.churchpublishing.org

Cover design by Jenn Kopec, 2Pug Design
Typeset by Rose Design

Library of Congress Cataloging-in-Publication Data

A record of this book is available from the Library of Congress.
ISBN-13: 978-0-8192-3293-9 (pbk.)
ISBN-13: 978-0-8192-3294-6 (ebook)

Printed in the United States of America

Beating the Boundaries

The Church God Is Calling Us to Be

John Spicer

Morehouse Publishing
NEW YORK

Contents

Acknowledgments

Many heads, hearts, hands, and wallets made this book possible. At the risk of forgetting someone, I want to thank the community of faithful people and institutions whose voices you will hear in the following pages and whose support enabled me to bring them together.

First are the people of St. Andrew's Episcopal Church in Kansas City, Missouri, and my colleagues there. The vestry was very supportive of my sabbatical time away and the focus of my study, and the church supported the project financially, too. Among the good people of St. Andrew's, I'm particularly indebted to:

- Stephen Rock, who served as senior warden and uncompensated consultant for three years and was my partner in shifting the culture of St. Andrew's toward collaborative leadership and missional focus. Great thanks also to Mary Heausler, who served as junior warden for two years. Their roles were taxing anyway, but both Steve and Mary shouldered additional burden during my sabbatical time.

- Gregory Bentz and Kathy Fowler, who served as senior warden and junior warden, respectively, once I returned from sabbatical and actually had to write the book. I'm grateful for their wisdom, support, and encouragement throughout this process.

- The Revs. Anne Hutcherson and Marcus Halley, my fellow priests at St. Andrew's, and the Ven. Bruce Bower, deacon (and archdeacon of the Diocese of West Missouri). Their commitment to their work, in time and heart, is tremendous—and then I took off for four months, leaving them with even more to bear. Thanks to them, I could leave and not worry (much) about what I might find when I returned.

- Mary Sanders, administrative assistant to the clergy at St. Andrew's, who has been tremendously patient with me as I wrote this book and found myself able to remember even less than I usually do.
- The members of my sabbatical committee at St. Andrew's: Rock, Heausler, Bentz, John Walker, Sean Kim, and Elaine Crider, whose encouragement and good questions shaped the sabbatical project proposal.

I'm also deeply grateful to those who provided funding for the project:

- The Louisville Institute (*www.louisville-institute.org*), which awarded me a Pastoral Study Project grant in 2013.
- The M B Krupp Foundation in Lenexa, Kansas, and its president, Gary A. Smith.
- St. Andrew's Episcopal Church, which invested in the project from its operating budget.

Perhaps the greatest blessing of this study has been the opportunity to meet and hear the stories of about ninety people across the nine congregations I visited. Not every interview resulted in a quote on the following pages, but many did—and all fleshed out the stories of the Holy Spirit's movement in their contexts. The following people are the voices of this book:

- **Boston:** the Very Rev. Jep Streit, the Rev. Canon Stephanie Spellers, Isaac Everett, the Rev. Trisha de Beer, the Rev. Marsha Hoecker, Loren Gary, James Van Looy, Shane Montoya, Mary Beth Mills Curran, Isaac Martinez, Derek Knox, Annie Kurdzeil, and Michael Zahniser.
- **Denver:** the Rt. Rev. Peter Eaton, Kate Eaton, the Rev. Jadon Hartsuff, the Rev. Elizabeth Randall, Missy Bell, Amy Beeson, Priscilla Shand, Bunny Low, Suni Devitt, Andy Devitt, and Larry Kueter.
- **Portland, Oregon:** the Rev. Karen Ward, Nathan Keith, Rob Stoltz, Philipos Ghaly, Leo Schuman, Justin Morgan, and Edna Hoesch.

- **Seattle:** the Rt. Rev. Melissa Skelton, Paul Steinke, Mark Taylor, the Rev. Samuel Torvend, Laura Griffin, Daryl Schlick, Loren Peters, Karin Stevens, Martin Pommerenke, and Pam Peterson.

- **Richmond, Virginia:** the Rev. Wallace Adams-Riley, the Rev. Melanie Mullen, Brian Levey, Beth Burton, Nick Courtney, Sam Jackson, and Maritza Mercado Pechin.

- **St. Mary's County, Maryland:** the Rev. Greg Syler, the Rev. Erin Betz-Shank, the Rev. John Ball, the Rev. Sherrill Page (posthumously), Eva Thompson, Tom McCarthy, Phil Horne, Les Taylor, and Tom DeSelms.

- **Tewkesbury, England:** the Rev. Paul Williams, the Rev. Wendy Ruffle, Graham Finch, Jean Day, Malcolm Gribble, Margaret Gribble, John Jeffreys, Sue Palmer, Lara Bloom, and the members of the Celebrate! Planning Group, who wish to remain anonymous.

- **London:** the Rev. Henry Kendal, the Rev. Helen Shannon, Sam Markey, Helen Davidson, Linda Cherry, Josie Poulter, Vivienne Chart, Liz Kovar, Lorraine Hills, and Vanessa Elsley.

- **Manchester, England:** the Rev. Nick Bundock, the Rev. Ben Edson, José Hacking, Jason Powell, Ann Hillier, Vicki Long, Beth Dickinson, Jon Parkin, Helen Leach, and Ben Jones.

And in London, thanks particularly to the Rev. Ian Mobsby, author and founder of the Moot Community, for making time to speak with me despite a scheduling snafu.

Thanks also to these people who provided direction and support in project planning:

- The Rev. Thomas Brackett, missioner for new church starts and missional initiatives for The Episcopal Church.
- The Rev. Canon Dr. Andrew Braddock, director of mission and ministry for the Church of England's Diocese of Gloucester.
- The Rev. Dr. Steven R. Rottgers, canon to the ordinary for the Episcopal Diocese of West Missouri.

My greatest thanksgiving goes to my wife, Ann Spicer, who traveled with me on most of the sabbatical visits and who has traveled alongside me for twenty-six years of marriage. There is nothing better than having your best friend also be your spouse. I thank her for her incredible patience through the planning and writing process, for her proofreading of a book that probably wouldn't have ended up on her bedside table, and for her understanding as I fell asleep on the couch more evenings than I would have liked.

And of course, in and through all of the above—thanks and glory be to God, "who by the power at work within us is able to accomplish abundantly far more than all we can ask or imagine" (Eph. 3:20).

Introduction

LET ME TELL YOU WHO I'M NOT. I am not a church-growth expert. I'm not an academic. I'm not a consultant. I've served as a parish priest for the past fourteen years in the Episcopal Diocese of West Missouri, a small diocese smack in the middle of fly-over country. I serve in Kansas City, which is a wonderful, interesting place but doesn't exactly have the hip cachet of Seattle or Brooklyn. So, you might well ask, why am I writing about "the Church God is calling us to be"?

I started my career in journalism. I'm just old enough that in my first job out of college in 1987, as a copy editor with the *Courier* in Waterloo, Iowa, old guys in the composition room were still running paper copy through hot waxers, cutting it with Exacto knives, and pasting it up on wooden tables. But I didn't stay in newspapers long enough to make the digital switch. Instead, I got the opportunity to be speechwriter and deputy press secretary for the governor of Missouri. Concerned I might lose my soul as well as my mind in politics, I found my way out, this time into medical writing and editing. At one point, I could spell any anesthetic agent you could name (though I'd had a total of one biology class in high school and college). From the practice-management journal of the American Academy of Family Physicians, I found God taking me to seminary (Seminary of the Southwest in Austin, Texas). And from there, I've served a grand total of two congregations: a small mission in Springfield, Missouri, which I closed, and St. Andrew's Episcopal in Kansas City. It's not exactly a résumé that says "church guru."

So let me tell you who I am: I'm a reporter of Good News who also gets involved in the story. I love to hear and share the experiences of real, live people who do amazing, godly things. Apparently something from my journalism classes stuck.

So, in 2014, I was blessed with a sabbatical to study nine congregations in The Episcopal Church and the Church of England
that were doing amazing, godly things. In their own ways, they
were pairing new expressions of ministry with their inherited
expressions—not turning away from who they'd been (some for
centuries) but turning toward the movement of the Holy Spirit.
In their own contexts, they heard the Spirit calling them to look
beyond the practices and expectations of church "the way we've
always done it" *without* leaving those ways behind. That both/
and approach appealed to me because of my own wiring. I'm
a member of what Professor Charlie Cook at Seminary of the
Southwest called "the radical middle"—a *via media*, big-tent
kind of guy. My heart tells me God is found most often in the
messiness of the middle, where you have to engage with issues
and people you might just as soon avoid, but you're better for it,
in the end.

I have to admit, there wasn't a lot of science in selecting the
congregations to study. I wanted to find a range that fleshed out
the Church's breadth—large and small, urban and rural, high-
church and low-church, American and English. The English perspective was important because the fresh expressions movement
has been well underway there for more than a decade, so their
experience surely had something to teach us across the pond. I
spoke with the Rev. Thomas Brackett, missioner for new church
starts and missional initiatives for The Episcopal Church, and he
gave me several good leads. Beyond that, networking coupled
with "the grace of God and sheer awkwardness," as my mother
likes to say, led me to identify the following places to visit during
my sabbatical:

- St. Paul's Cathedral in Boston and the Crossing;
- St. John's Cathedral in Denver and the Wilderness;
- St. Andrew and All Souls Church in Portland, Oregon;
- St. Paul's Church in Seattle and its 5 p.m. Community;
- St. Paul's Church in Richmond, Virginia, and Center;
- Three small parishes in St. Mary's County, Maryland—
  St. George's, Ascension, and Trinity—together offering new

expressions of ministry and struggling to create
collaborative governance;

- St. James & Emmanuel Church in Manchester, England, and
  Abide;
- St. Barnabas Church in London and Church@Five; and
- Tewkesbury Abbey in Tewkesbury, England, and Celebrate!

This book tells their stories and draws from them five questions for congregations to ask as they hear God's call to push past the boundaries they've inherited. As everyone knows, we can no longer just be quaint little red-doored expressions of Anglican sacramental life. Nor can we be the denomination of the presidents, the country club at prayer, relying on the power of American Christendom and waiting for the right people to come our way. God is calling all of our congregations to break down the boundaries we've unwittingly marked out between ourselves and people hungrier than ever for the true bread that came down from heaven, the Word that brings life. Existing congregations can move in new ways without leaving their histories or their DNA behind. And we don't all have to put on cool, emerging church services or hire young clergy in skinny jeans. We have to listen both to the contexts in which God has placed us and to the call of Scripture and tradition to hear how God is asking us to explore our boundaries and build relationships with the people we find there. We have to ask ourselves hard questions about congregational DNA, whom we might reach, what sort of new ministry the Spirit might be inspiring, how we'll lead and govern it, and how we'll define success and failure.

And then, like these nine congregations I visited, we have to act. We have to live as apostles, the hands and feet of the Jesus movement, beating our boundaries and taking the risk to engage with new people in new ways—without losing our bearings and forgetting the path back home.

A few thoughts about the chapters ahead: The book begins with an overview of where The Episcopal Church finds itself, the fresh expressions and emerging church movements, and "beating the bounds" as a symbol we might reclaim and reinterpret for

congregations and their contexts today. Chapter 2 profiles the nine
congregations I studied, telling their stories of creating and sus-
taining (or not) new expressions of ministry. The next five chapters offer questions congregations should answer as they step out
on their own boundary-beating journeys, as well as guidance from
people who've paved the way:

- Where's the mission in your DNA?
- Whom are you trying to reach—and how?
- What expression of ministry is God trying to create?
- How will you empower strong leadership and plan for
  governance?
- How will you identify success and failure?

The eighth chapter suggests we might strengthen the missional orientation of inherited ministries by applying these same five questions to them.

Although the congregations I profile are part of The Episcopal Church or the Church of England, the principles aren't
specific to my denomination. Any mainline congregation dealing
with life post-Christendom will find a familiar narrative here.

When I came back from my sabbatical, some parishioners
asked me if I'd found the model for St. Andrew's—a Holy Grail of
how to practice the "both/and" of established congregations raising up new expressions of ministry. In my visits, I sometimes also
found myself naively wondering, "Which is the best model?" Of
course, there's no such thing—and that's part of the point. In the
same way that the final answer about the doctrine of the Trinity is
"It's a mystery," the final answer about the practice of ministry is,
"It's contextual." But, in a larger sense, what I saw was the same
journey being taken by faithful people in vastly different contexts.
The explorers, the gear, the landscape, and the accents changed,
but their stories share a common narrative.

May our journeys be as faithful, and as blessed, as the journeys I've been blessed to narrate.

1

Beating the Bounds, Beating the Boundaries

"O LORD, you are my portion and my cup; it is you who uphold my lot. My boundaries enclose a pleasant land; indeed, I have a goodly heritage." —Psalm 16:5–6 (Book of Common Prayer)

IN THIS AGE OF DIGITAL EVERYTHING, one of the most seemingly out-of-touch observances on the Episcopal liturgical calendar must be the Rogation Days—the Monday, Tuesday, and Wednesday before Ascension Day. On these days, we ask (*rogare* in Latin) God's blessing on agriculture and, more recently, on wider expressions of commerce and industry. The practice comes from imperial Rome, when citizens would walk to a grove outside the city to pray to the god Robigus to protect their crops. As Christianity syncretized Roman practices, the Christian God took Robigus's place in the ritual. In the fifth century, the bishop of Vienne in Gaul introduced a three-day rite seeking God's protection after a series of earthquakes. The priest would lead his people into the fields to beg God's blessing on the land and their crops. The observance spread in Europe, taking place on the three days before Ascension Day. Pope Gregory the Great formalized the observance and fixed a date of April 25; and in 707, the Council of Cloveshoo introduced the Rogation Days into English liturgical life. After prayers at the parish church, the priest led the people through their village and literally around the geographic parish, singing hymns and offering

1

Scripture readings and homilies. Crosses, banners, and standards led the people in procession (Stilgoe 49).

In England, the festival morphed from a liturgical to a geographic exercise as well, combining supplication and thanksgiving with the practicalities of marking parish boundaries in a day before surveying. During the processions, people would literally beat the bounds, striking trees, rocks, and pathways to remind themselves, and those in neighboring parishes, where the boundaries lay (di Bonaventura 117). Participants in the festivities would also bump children against significant boundary-marking trees, hit them on the head, or dunk them head first into rivers as aids to memory; and villagers would play tug-of-war with people from neighboring parishes across boundary streams. Clerical instruction included not just God's sovereignty over the land but the sin of moving human boundary markers, illustrated through passages like Deuteronomy 27:17. Each parish vicar had a stake in the process: Defining the parish boundaries, and preventing encroachment by other parishes, made clear which tithes he would be entitled to receive (Stilgoe 50). By the seventeenth century, with increasing population and common land being threatened by the enclosure movement, careful boundary definitions became even more important. As landscape historian John R. Stilgoe notes, "Religion, law, and folk custom all served to define the village outline and secure the community landscape from old and new forms of external disruption. . . . Rogation perambulations ensured every villager of his particular location within the kingdom; they defined his community space and sanctified his personal property" (Stilgoe 51).

Today, beating the bounds in a Rogation procession carries theological weight as a sign of our enduring connection with, and responsibility for, the good earth God has given us. It's also a great opportunity for some quaint reveling in Anglican tradition—what longtime Episcopalian or Anglican doesn't love a good procession? And it's even more fun outside. Churches in England and the United States have renewed the practice and shared it with the world on social media. (Search for "beating the bounds" and "rogation procession" on YouTube.) Like our English spiritual forebears, perhaps we value knowing where our boundaries lie as God's people in a given place, with our space clearly defined and pleasingly sanctified. Of course, the shadow side of well-defined boundaries is the temptation to remain within them, seemingly safe (or at least shielded) from forces that threaten the church from outside.

Despite the rural heritage of western Missouri, where I serve, the Rogation Days aren't a highlight on most churches' liturgical calendars. In my first congregation—Church of the Good Shepherd, a small mission in Springfield, Missouri—I decided we'd try it. I donned a cassock and surplice, took up the processional cross, and led several intrepid members around the church grounds. We stopped along the way to hear Scripture, thank God for the abundance of creation, and pray for seasonable weather and the fruits of the earth. What I remember most was feeling exceptionally self-conscious as we pretended to be a quaint English country church marking its parish boundaries. Our neighbors, in this buckle on the Bible Belt, probably thought we were crazy. Or, more likely, they never noticed at all.

What I missed at Good Shepherd was the opportunity to teach about our little liturgical procession. Beyond naming our role as stewards of creation and celebrating "all good gifts around us," we were living out DNA we didn't even know we had. That mission congregation had been founded eleven years before I arrived. Its initial energy had been about using praise music, charismatic worship, and the Alpha course to attract people who didn't know the Episcopal tradition. Unfortunately, by the time I arrived, that energy had dissipated into a small circle of comfort where most of the congregation was happy to receive the blessings of healing and community without much interest in reaching anyone else. We tried to attract new members to worship and special events, and the parishioners were very welcoming when outsiders arrived. But they were content to open their doors rather than moving outside them. The mindset mirrored our quaint little Rogation procession: Our "boundaries enclose[d] a pleasant land" (Psalm 16:6, BCP), and the congregation was happy staying within them. Not surprisingly, Good Shepherd closed a couple of years later.

It's a mindset common in liturgical sacramental congregations, Episcopal and otherwise. We do what we do; we're happy when others come by; and we're proud when we do a good job of welcoming them on a Sunday morning. That's absolutely vital, and hard, work—and it's only a good start. We can't just open the doors to let people in; we have to see our boundaries—physical and emotional—as starting lines for moving out to engage the people around us. And the mission field is ripe. The end of American Christendom has left a remarkable percentage of the population at work, in bed, or at soccer on Sunday mornings. The "churchless" comprise 43 percent of the U.S. population, according to the Barna Group. That breaks down into 33 percent of the population being de-churched (having left a church at some point) and 10 percent being unchurched (having never been part of a faith community) (Barna and Kinnaman 6).

As the saying goes, God's church doesn't have a mission; God's mission has a church. In Matthew's gospel, Jesus brings the story to a close by sending the first apostles out beyond their circle: "Go therefore and make disciples of all nations . . ." (28:19). The apostolic church took up that call and turned a Jewish sect into a world religion. The apostolic church today is still "sent to carry out Christ's mission to all people," a mission of "restor[ing] all people to unity with God and each other in Christ" (BCP 854–55). Beyond words in the Bible and the prayer book, Episcopalians and Anglicans are living and speaking the call. The Rev. Stephanie Spellers, founder of the emerging community the Crossing in Boston (see p. 16) and now canon to the Presiding Bishop for evangelism and reconciliation, says a missional church goes about its work using a missionary's tools in its own context: "listening, being present, building relationships, and becoming companions within a community, especially across boundaries of difference." This "means stepping across a boundary in order to partner with whatever is emerging in your context, even—and especially—when it entails moving into a place that your ministry has rarely ventured into before" (Spellers, "Monocultural Church in a Hybrid World" 20).

That call for The Episcopal Church to engage the world is not exactly news. Just in my merely fifty years as a cradle Episcopalian,

I can remember ventures in mission and decades of evangelism. Congregations have tried visitor Sundays and renewal weekends and praise services. Our best efforts haven't exactly borne bountiful fruit. You don't have to be a statistician to understand the numbers from our own research office—decades of decreasing membership and worship attendance, resulting in an Episcopal Church that reports about 1.96 million members and 1.5 million communicants in good standing (Office of General Convention), down 43 percent from its peak of 3.43 million members in 1966 (Episcopal Church). So, for many Episcopal congregations, the functional mission is survival. Firmly rooted in American Christendom, and given a false sense of security by the Baby Boom and social expectations of church membership of the mid-twentieth century, Episcopal congregations now see traditional patterns of membership, attendance, and financial support going the way of the landline phone.

None of that is news either. But after a while, the litanies of decline begin to feel like indictments of apathy or incompetence. If we—especially ordained leaders—just "did it right," we could see the growth they're seeing at some of our competitor churches down the street. Church-growth strategies sometimes leave Episcopalians feeling like they're being asked to crash a party wearing someone else's clothes: If we'd just learn the secrets of the "successful" churches and imitate them, we could imitate their growth, too. If we just advertised more, or welcomed people better, or offered more "singable" music, or projected the lyrics on screens, or preached more sermon series, or had more small groups, or served better coffee, or . . . Everyone has a solution the priest and vestry should try.

Expecting a congregation to turn itself into something it's not doesn't seem like a great strategy for success. But what about becoming more of what we already are? God is calling us to claim a bigger sense of "church," to see church not as an institution but a movement—"the Episcopal branch of the Jesus movement," as Presiding Bishop Michael Curry likes to say (Curry). God is calling us once again to explore the boundaries of our parishes but with a new intention. Though many congregations define boundaries that offer security and comfort, God is asking us to beat the bounds in a new way—pressing our boundaries to open passageways of permeability that can help our religious institutions remember who we are by engaging with the neighbors and networks around us. In one local congregation after another, The Episcopal Church can express missional DNA in ways we know and in ways we're just beginning to know, following the Holy Spirit's lead in being relational, sacramental, Trinitarian communities, both as God has gifted us to be and as God is gifting us to become. Doing so, we follow Jesus's lead, embodying God's kingdom "like the master of a household who brings out of his treasure what is new and what is old" (Matt. 13:52).

Over the past ten to fifteen years in The Episcopal Church and especially in the Church of England, some pioneers have been exploring this path—not a new path exactly because it draws on who Anglicans have been as much as imagining who Anglicans may become. The path has carried different names in different contexts: mission-shaped church, emerging church, emergent church, fresh expressions. No label has captured this movement of the Holy Spirit fully, and each term has picked up baggage while losing power through overuse. But these new expressions of church tap deeply into the Anglican ethos—embracing embodied, participatory worship; being open to the treasures of the liturgical tradition; putting relationship ahead of doctrinal unity; creating authentic community that starts with belonging, not believing; and building people's capacity to live faithfully in ambiguity and wrestle with hard questions, rather than teaching them the "right" answers.

Mission-Shaped Church and Fresh Expressions in the UK

In 2004, the Church of England—Anglicanism's great bastion of tradition and centralized authority—charted a new course in mission by arguing for a rich diversity of church expressions. The *Mission-Shaped Church* report was a wake-up call to the declining role of the Anglican Church in British life, as well as the need for new strategies to engage the de-churched and the unchurched. Then-Archbishop of Canterbury Rowan Williams called for intentional development of a "mixed economy" of Anglican ecclesial practice, "fresh expressions and 'inherited' forms of church existing alongside each other, within the same denomination, in relationships of mutual respect and support" ("What Is the Mixed Economy?"). The Church of England defines fresh expressions as "form[s] of church for our changing culture, established primarily for the benefit of people who are not yet members of any church. [They] will come into being through principles of listening, service, contextual mission and making disciples" ("What Is a Fresh Expression of Church?"). According to the *Mission-Shaped Church* report, the term "fresh expressions" includes both existing churches that are renewing or redirecting their ministry, as well as other efforts to go out and "discover what will emerge when the gospel is immersed in the mission context." The report also acknowledges that the term is problematic because it "does not easily differentiate between the[se] two realities" (Archbishop's Council on Mission and Public Affairs 34).

A key mark of fresh expressions in the British context is the direction of missional engagement. The Church of England's Fresh Expressions website argues that inherited forms of church expect people to take the initiative to come to them, which establishes the church's worldview as normative. "Fresh expressions have a 'we'll come to you' mindset instead," the website explains. "They start not with an invitation ('Come to us on our terms'), but with an offer ('We're willing to come to you, serve you and stay with you. If you want, we'll also help you to be church in a way that suits you—in your style, not ours')" ("What Is a Fresh Expression of Church?"). So, fresh expressions take the church out of its known and comfortable contexts to "make the love of God known in an increasingly secular society," according to pioneer-ministry trainers David Goodhew, Andrew Roberts, and Michael Volland. "They have a deep sense of being sent, of apostolicity" (Goodhew, Roberts, and Volland 76).

That missional offer is being extended in a wide variety of settings in the UK. Pioneer ministers (as those leading these communities are known) are raising up new expressions of church in cafés and workplaces; among mothers' groups, young adults, and older people; among the poor and in neomonastic communities; in urban centers and small villages; and even online ("Examples"). Ministers pioneering these efforts would claim all points on the theological spectrum, and they come from catholic, charismatic, broad-church, and monastic backgrounds. In that great range, some see the hand and heart of God reaching out to God's children. "It is this diversity in particular that suggests we may be truly seeing something of the *missio dei* unfold" (Goodhew, Roberts, and Volland 73).

A mixed-economy church doesn't intend to replace inherited forms of worship and community, but the older forms are being held to a renewed standard of outward-directedness. "The challenge is not to force everything into the familiar mold; but neither is it to tear up the rulebook and start from scratch (as if that were ever possible or realistic)," Williams writes. "What makes the situation interesting is that we are going to have to live with variety" (Archbishop's Council on Mission and Public Affairs v). Writer Brian McLaren takes it one step further, seeing the benefits of competition in the mixed economy where churches "create new wineskins while the existing wineskins [are] still in use [and] compete with themselves (in a non-competitive way)" (McLaren 19). That process strengthens both kinds of expressions, says British theologian Lincoln Harvey, with "pioneering practitioners drawing lessons from both past and present" and "new ideas for mission . . . being folded back into inherited models of Church, thereby establishing new and dynamic enterprises within the context of the local parish" (Harvey 95).

Emerging Church in the US

Much the same missional heartbeat impels the emerging church movement in the United States. The different terms—fresh expressions and emerging church—reflect different contexts on each side of the Atlantic. Whereas fresh expressions have been spurred and resourced by the Church of England, the emerging church in the United States is decentralized, taking shape indigenously and with little coordination. Spellers writes that the two movements have reinforced each other without ever quite coming together: "In spirit, they have always been intimately connected, with pioneers and thinkers collaborating like two streams running parallel, sometimes jumping the banks and flowing on the other side, only to return with fresh ideas and bigger questions" (Spellers, "From the Editors" xiii).

Emergence is easier to describe than to define. Church historian and sociologist Phyllis Tickle writes of the "the Great Emergence," the present seismic shift in Western culture and religion, as the next step in a five-hundred-year sociological pattern of transformation following in the footsteps of the Great Schism and the Protestant Reformation. Religiously, the Great Emergence "presents in real life as emergings, emergents, missionals, neo-monastics, hyphenateds, fresh expressions among others." These are "kindred member-parts of a new form of Christianity . . . born out of the pervasive and abiding distrust and suspicion in our times of any institution." Emergence Christians believe community trumps religious institutions. But some want "common ground between the suspect institution and the vitality of the autonomous community," and they "seek to create worshiping, serving communities that reverence the aesthetic and experience of the institution without compromising the autonomy of the group." These are the "hyphenateds"—Anglimergents, Presbymergents, Luthermergents, etc. (Tickle 61–63).

Writer and theologian Tony Jones points out the challenge in defining American emergent Christianity, given that emergents don't share polity, worship style, theology, or a central organizing structure. Instead, emergents self-identify with a movement that reinterprets inherited churches' priorities, values, and theology for postmodern people (Jones 4–5). Jones identifies the movement's core practices as regular Holy Communion; an ambiguous informality of worship; collaborative preaching; highly interactive community; hospitality experienced as authentic welcome, connection, and safety; theological openness; artistic creation as holy practice; a high doctrine of lay involvement (the priesthood of all believers);

and sacred space that reflects a relational aesthetic as it pays homage to tradition (Jones 100–121).

Other writers have identified similar marks of the emerging church. From interviews with emerging church participants in the United States and Europe, Eddie Gibbs and Ryan Bolger distilled these nine characteristics: living according to Jesus's model, transforming the secular world, practicing community intentionally, welcoming people outside the group, serving and sharing generously, participating in God's world as producers, creating as an expression of having been created in God's image, sharing leadership widely without a strong need to control, and merging ancient and contemporary spiritual practice (Gibbs and Bolger 44–45).

On those marks of emerging church life, Ian Mobsby sees fingerprints of the Holy Trinity itself. Mobsby is a priest, writer, and teacher on fresh expressions and the emerging church. He's also the founder of Moot, a neomonastic community that offers worship, spiritual formation, a haven from urban life, and outstanding coffee in central London. In these core values of the emerging church, Mobsby sees two fundamental aspects of God's being: perichoresis (the mutually interdependent and nonhierarchical relationship among the three persons of the Trinity) and kenosis (God's radically self-giving love ultimately manifested in Jesus's redemptive suffering and death). Mobsby believes it's no accident emerging expressions of church take the shape they do, arguing that the emerging church models "spiritual community that reflects the very nature of the Trinitarian Godhead. The Holy Spirit is drawing those seeking missional and contemporary expressions of church for our postmodern consumerist context to experiment with forms of church drawing on a perichoretic model" (Mobsby, *God Unknown: The Trinity in Contemporary Spirituality and Mission* 75).

In a perichoretic and kenotic church—one rooted in relationships and self-giving—the first work is not to form belief but to form community. As Diana Butler Bass argues in *Christianity After Religion*, the European and American church has long assumed that religious commitment begins with intellectual assent to a set of doctrines—an approach that doesn't speak well to a culture increasingly suspicious of religious institutions and likely to see doctrine as a tool of exclusion and control. The growing "spiritual but not religious" in American culture identify far more with an experience of faith in community than a religious institution's branded version of divine truth. So, Bass argues, a church seeking to take part in God's mission to those outside itself should reverse the priorities, moving away from "believe, become, belong" and embracing "belong, become, believe." Bass sees "experiential Christianity" as the key to churches' offering a way of life rather than membership in a religious organization. "We are; we act; we know," she writes. "Belonging, behaving, and believing—shifted back to their proper and ancient order. This is the shape of awakened Christianity, a faith that is a deeply spiritual religion . . . the Great Returning of Christianity back toward what Jesus preached" (Bass 214). The Church of England's fresh expressions manual concurs, noting that "people don't enter the faith head-first. They don't begin with belief, then join the church and finally start to change their behavior. More typical is that they become believers as a result of being part of a Christian community," either in the order of "belong, believe, behave" or "belong, behave, believe" ("Discipleship Starts Where People Are").

Mobsby agrees, framing it in terms of what the church needs to get right and in what order. In modernity, the church put orthodoxy first, but spiritual formation has to start with orthopathy, Mobsby says—a growing sense of wholeness. The next step is orthopraxis, following Christ in what we do. "All of that leads to orthodoxy, and you can't jump to orthodoxy unless you've worked through the other two. That's why there are so many de-churched people in the UK, because we've been obsessed with courses and orthodoxy" (Mobsby, Personal interview).

A number of writers argue that the Anglican tradition, and The Episcopal Church specifically, is among the most fertile American ground for the emerging church movement to take root and blossom. Anglican wiring aligns well with what draws emergents into relationship with God. The Rev. Karen Ward (see p. 31), one of the leaders of the Anglimergent movement, drew on this alignment when she founded Church of the Apostles in Seattle in 2002. "I was convinced that Anglo-Catholic ritual, practice and sacramental mysticism—when brought into dialogue with contemporary art, culture and media, in the context of a welcoming and 'culturally fluent' community—could provide space and place for postmodern seekers to fall in love with God, form community with one another and then practice extending God's love to the surrounding neighbourhood," she writes (Ward 166). On a broader scale, Tickle agrees that Anglicanism is a rich vault for new church expressions: "The treasures of Anglicanism were never ours, of course, though we have often been pleased to think so. They are instead the treasures of the faith deposited into our history for safekeeping until just such a time as this" (Tickle 72).

But I Already Have a Church . . .

That sounds like good news for Episcopal church planters, but the vast majority of Episcopal leaders have their hands full with their own congregations. So how can existing congregations step into "such a time as this"? Some are doing just that—discerning how God is intending them to be church in a new day and breaking down boundaries they have largely built around themselves. These congregations aren't moving away from familiar patterns of Anglican life. Instead, they've discerned a missional call to connect with their communities and embody God's kingdom by offering both what is "old" and what is "new." While existing congregations sometimes find themselves bound by longstanding patterns—controlling from the top down, speaking from the center, producing programs to meet perceived needs, and focusing on the people they've traditionally served—some are finding ways to open up those boundaries, embracing bottom-up collaboration, learning from voices at the edge, creating space for authentic relationships to grow, and focusing on the people God has placed nearby as well as their traditional membership pool.

New expressions of ministry in existing congregations are taking the Church of England's "mixed economy" model to the micro level. That requires not just missional passion but a willingness to change some of the structures and presumptions we've inherited as an institutional church. For Mobsby—who began the Moot Community as a fresh expression within St. Matthew's, Westminster, in London—it means congregations must recover a sense of *apostolos* empowered by the Holy Spirit, "the gathering and sending of the people of God." To practice mission in an apostolic way takes three ancient-future mindsets: First, mission must be relational rather than programmatic or marketing-oriented. "If you're engaging with spiritual seekers, the personal approach is vital because faith for them is all about experience." Second, new expressions of church need a seat at the congregational leadership table and a voice in governance. And third, congregations trying new expressions of ministry need to give themselves permission to risk. "We have to know that one in five things might survive, and four in five will not," Mobsby said. "When we do mission and start something, it seems we've got to keep it going for the next thousand years; otherwise, it's a failure. We need to get away from that" (Mobsby, Personal interview).

So, on the ground, what does it look like to create new expressions of church alongside church as we've known it? What happens when we beat the bounds not to mark where parish responsibility and authority stop but, instead, to mark where our journey begins?

References

Archbishop's Council on Mission and Public Affairs. *Mission-Shaped Church: Church Planting and Fresh Expressions in a Changing Context.* New York: Seabury Books, 2010.

Barna, George, and David Kinnaman. *Churchless: Understanding Today's Unchurched and How to Connect with Them.* Carol Stream, IL: Tyndale House Publishers, 2014.

Bass, Diana Butler. *Christianity After Religion: The End of the Church and the Birth of a New Spiritual Awakening.* New York: Harper Collins, 2012.

Curry, Michael. "Presiding Bishop Michael Curry: This Is the Jesus Movement, and We Are The Episcopal Church, the Episcopal Branch of Jesus' Movement in This World." Last modified November 2, 2015. Accessed January 2, 2016. *http://www.episcopalchurch.org/posts/*

publicaffairs/presiding-bishop-michael-curry-jesus-movement-and-we-are-episcopal-church.

di Bonaventura, Allegra. "Beating the Bounds: Property and Perambulation in Early New England." *Yale Journal of Law & the Humanities* 19, no. 2 (2007): 115–48.

"Discipleship Starts Where People Are." Accessed December 30, 2015. *http://www.freshexpressions.org.uk/guide/discipleship/starts.*

"Episcopal Church." Accessed January 2, 2016. *http://www.thearda.com/Denoms/D_849.asp.*

"Examples." Accessed December 28, 2015. *http://www.freshexpressions.org.uk/guide/examples.*

Gibbs, Eddie, and Ryan K. Bolger. *Emerging Church: Creating Christian Communities in Postmodern Culture.* Grand Rapids, MI: Baker, 2005.

Goodhew, David, Andrew Roberts, and Michael Volland. *Fresh! An Introduction to Fresh Expressions of Church and Pioneer Ministry.* London: SCM Press, 2012.

Harvey, Lincoln. "How Serious Is It Really? The Mixed Economy and the Light-Hearted Long Haul." In *Ancient Faith, Future Mission: Fresh Expressions of Church and the Kingdom of God*, edited by Graham Cray, Aaron Kennedy, and Ian Mobsby, 95–105. Norwich, UK: Canterbury Press, 2012.

Jones, Tony. *The Church Is Flat: The Relational Ecclesiology of the Emerging Church Movement.* Minneapolis, MN: JoPa Group, 2011.

McLaren, Brian. "One, Holy, Catholic, and Fresh?" In *Ancient Faith, Future Mission: Fresh Expressions in the Sacramental Tradition*, edited by Steven Croft, Ian Mobsby, and Stephanie Spellers, 9–19. New York: Seabury Books, 2010.

Mobsby, Ian. *God Unknown: The Trinity in Contemporary Spirituality and Mission.* Norwich, UK: Canterbury Press, 2012.

———. Personal interview by John Spicer. October 20, 2014.

Office of General Convention, The Episcopal Church. "Table of Statistics of the Episcopal Church From 2014 Parochial Reports." January 2016. *http://www.episcopalchurch.org/files/2014_table_of_statistics_english.pdf.*

"Rogation Days." Accessed December 31, 2015. *http://www.episcopalchurch.org/library/glossary/rogation-days.*

Spellers, Stephanie. "From the Editors." In *Ancient Faith, Future Mission: Fresh Expressions in the Sacramental Tradition*, edited by

Steven Croft, Ian Mobsby, and Stephanie Spellers, xiii–xv. New York: Seabury Books, 2010.

———. "Monocultural Church in a Hybrid World." In *The Hyphenateds: How Emergence Christianity Is Re-Traditioning Mainline Practices*, edited by Phil Snider,12–25. St. Louis: Chalice Press, 2011.

Stilgoe, John R. "Jack-O'-Lanterns to Surveyors: The Secularization of Landscape Boundaries." In *Landscape and Images*, 47–63. Charlottesville: University of Virginia Press, 2005.

Tickle, Phyllis. "Changes and a Changeless Faith." In *Ancient Faith, Future Mission: Fresh Expressions of Church and the Kingdom of God*, edited by Graham Cray, Aaron Kennedy, and Ian Mobsby, 59–76. Norwich, UK: Canterbury Press, 2012.

Ward, Karen. "A Story of Anglimergence: Community, Covenant, Eucharist and Mission at Church of the Apostles." In *Ancient Faith, Future Mission: Fresh Expressions in the Sacramental Traditions*, edited by Steven Croft, Ian Mobsby, and Stephanie Spellers, 165–70. New York: Seabury Books, 2010.

"What Is a Fresh Expression of Church?" Accessed December 28, 2015. *http://www.freshexpressions.org.uk/guide/about/whatis*.

"What Is the Mixed Economy?" Accessed December 28, 2015. *http://www.freshexpressions.org.uk/guide/about/mixedeconomy*.

2

Nine Stories of Beating
the Boundaries

"I . . . decided, after investigating everything carefully from
the very first, to write an orderly account for you, most excellent Theophilus." —Luke 1:3

IN 2014, AS PART OF A SABBATICAL study project supported
by the Louisville Institute, I visited nine Episcopal and Church of
England congregations, each of which had raised up a new expression of ministry. Here are their stories. They run the gamut—large
to small, urban to rural, Anglo-Catholic to evangelical. Their stories reflect the rich intersection of each congregation's unique gifts,
the needs of its context, and the creative power of the Holy Spirit
always to raise up new life among us.

St. Paul's Cathedral and the Crossing, Boston

Looking down the hill from the Massachusetts State House across
Boston Common to Tremont Street, you notice one façade that
seems out of place among the office buildings: a neoclassical structure with columns and a pediment above the portico. Where you
might expect to see reliefs of Roman soldiers returning from battle, you see instead the large white outline of a nautilus on a striking blue field—a "symbol of universal invitation and welcome"

adorning the Cathedral Church of St. Paul ("History and Mission"). At a glance, little about this sight says, "Episcopal cathedral." But welcome runs all through the cathedral's DNA, and that ethos has been breaking down boundaries in downtown Boston for decades.

A House of Prayer for All People

St. Paul's was established in 1818 as Boston's fourth Episcopal congregation. Ninety-four years later, when the Diocese of Massachusetts received a bequest to build a cathedral, Bishop William Lawrence opted to use the money for ministry instead and convert St. Paul's into a cathedral ("History and Mission"). From the beginning, the cathedral has seen itself as "a house of prayer for all people," said the Very Rev. John P. (Jep) Streit Jr., the cathedral's dean. Initially, "that meant economically," Streit said. The new cathedral removed the doors, and the rents, from St. Paul's box pews. "Everyone was welcome regardless of economic status or social class. And this place has lived into that" (Streit, Personal interview 1).

Today, St. Paul's is a cathedral of several congregations. The Sunday early service is an intimate Rite I Eucharist in a side chapel. The late-morning Rite II Eucharist brings 80 to 100. After lunch, a Cantonese Episcopal congregation of about 100 gathers for worship. On Thursday evenings, about 40 people gather as a fresh expression of church begun at the cathedral—the Crossing. And on Fridays, about 350 Muslims gather at the cathedral for Friday prayers.

The cathedral's most recent step in diversity is a step toward tradition. In 2013, St. Paul's merged with an Anglo-Catholic Episcopal congregation around the corner, St. John the Evangelist, which was about to close (Sukraw). The sale of St. John's property helped fund a $9 million renovation of the cathedral's worship space—including getting rid of the box pews. But the merger is also a way the cathedral can reach people whom it unintentionally, and ironically, hadn't welcomed before. "We pride ourselves on being a house of prayer for all people, and I thought, 'We're not very welcoming to traditional Episcopalians,'" Streit said. "They would have been uneasy here, and Anglo-Catholics wouldn't have felt welcome here at all" (Streit, Personal interview 1).

About a third of the cathedral congregation is homeless, Streit says, as are several of the people in liturgical roles on any given Sunday. "They're grateful there's a church that doesn't just tolerate them but where they're full members, where they're leaders, where on Sunday morning they're reading the lessons and carrying the cross," Streit said. "We'd be sunk without them" (Streit, Personal interview 2).

Organizing a Community, Then Worshiping

In 2005, a young leader put new flesh and bones on the cathedral's welcoming ethos using community-organizing principles to reach neighbors who hadn't felt welcomed in other churches. Before seminary, the Rev. Stephanie Spellers had been part of the cathedral, attending a young adult fellowship Streit had started. When Spellers came to the cathedral's staff after ordination, Streit suggested she renew the young adult ministry. Spellers pitched a different idea: "Create a fresh expression and build a community that would together discern what is the shape of Christian life in our context—younger, multicultural, downtown Boston, with a lot of students around," Spellers said (Spellers, Personal interview).

Spellers had just written *Radical Welcome*, so she came to the cathedral with a passion for connecting emerging generations with the Anglican tradition. She also came with background in community organizing, learned in a previous congregation and in seminary. "The lead organizer is supposed to facilitate the leadership of the people," Spellers explained. Rather than working from a top-down, follow-me model, the leader meets with people one-on-one to build relationships and spark new ones. "In those meetings, the organizer is listening for passion, concerns, what drives people to act and make a commitment to something greater than themselves," Spellers said. The organizer wants to learn "what are their gifts, what are their experiences, what are the intersections in their stories, what has God been up to, where have they seen God?" (Spellers, Personal interview).

In countless conversations, Spellers asked people what "fresh Christian community" would look like in downtown Boston:

"How would you be praying? Who would be gathered, and where? What experiences of God do you wish a Christian community could honor?" As she found people excited by the conversation, she invited them to help make that community real (Spellers, Personal interview).

But the dean and new priest weren't yet on the same page. Streit imagined Spellers was creating a new Sunday night service, and he wondered what was taking so long (Streit, Personal interview 1). But Spellers was seeing something more like an affiliated congregation. "The Crossing was not to be an evening service for the Cathedral," she said. "The original leadership team included only a couple from the cathedral congregation, by design. We weren't just creating an interesting service for people who already worshipped at the cathedral on Sundays. This was truly to be a missional effort" (Spellers, Personal interview).

After a few months of building a web of community, one coffee or beer at a time, Spellers invited her new connections, and a few people from the cathedral, to take part in "worship learning parties." At that time, Church of the Apostles (COTA), an Episcopal-Lutheran emerging church in Seattle, was in its early years; and Spellers invited its founder, the Rev. Karen Ward, to demonstrate COTA's worship in Boston. Participants included "downtown Boston people, students, people without a lot of money, and liturgy nuts," Spellers said. Afterward, Spellers invited them to help design worship for this new proto-church community. "We had thirty volunteers who said, 'I don't just want to attend something; I want to be part of creating something.' So those are the people you start with" (Spellers, Personal interview). The worship learning parties continued into 2006 as the Crossing came to find a worship style authentic to the community it was becoming. Spellers led the Crossing until 2012.

Indigenous Leadership, Radical Welcome

The Crossing's identity is about indigenous leadership and radical welcome. "It's not about starting a worship service," said Isaac Everett, the Crossing's minister of liturgical arts. "It's about planting a community" (Everett, Personal interview 2). Just as the Crossing invites people to help create something rather than attend something, it expects their gifts and voices to guide the community. Even in the Crossing's early years, Spellers worked hard to decentralize authority and invest members with leadership. "For the first three years, I didn't preach at the Crossing at all," she said. "I knew if I preached, then I'd be the only one trusted to proclaim the Gospel and they wouldn't become the group of disciples and leaders they need to be" (Spellers, Personal interview).

Everett shares in that leadership as a paid staff member. A composer and musician (his albums include *Rotation* and *Transmission*), seminary graduate, and author (*The Emergent Psalter*), Everett sees worship's ability to embody and prepare disciples to lead—or not. "Everything you do in worship forms you—and that's not necessarily a good thing," Everett explained. "If you're learning an instrument and you practice badly, you're going to learn bad habits" (Everett, Personal interview 2).

One bad habit from inherited church is professionalizing the proclamation of Good News. "In the rubrics of the Book of Common Prayer, only clergy are supposed to read the Gospel," Everett noted. "So you do that week after week after week, and it teaches that, if you're a layperson, it's not your job to proclaim the Gospel. Or perhaps, even worse, that you're not *worthy* to proclaim the Gospel." To undermine that pattern and build leadership throughout the community, Crossing worship includes the whole congregation chanting the Gospel, as well as preaching by laypeople five out of six weeks. "Where else are you going to learn how to tell your story and the story of God's love if you don't get an opportunity to practice [in worship]?" (Everett, Personal interview 2).

That leadership doesn't stop at the church door. The Crossing takes seriously equipping the saints for the work of ministry (Eph 4:12). "The laity are the ministers of the Church, and the ministry of the Church is to the world . . . not to the laity," Everett said. "The Crossing doesn't show up in order to be ministered to; the Crossing shows up to become ministers and then go change the world" (Everett, Personal interview 1).

The other clear mark of the Crossing's identity is radical welcome, which Spellers defines as shaping a congregation by welcoming "those who have been defined as The Other, pushed to the margins, cast out, silenced, and closeted" (Spellers, *Radical Welcome: Embracing God, The Other, and the Spirit of Transformation* 15). For at least one Crossing member, that looks like not having to fight for a place in the community. Annie Kurdzeil, who came into the Crossing in 2012, said, "This was the first church I ever went to where I saw a lesbian couple holding hands. It's not a fight you're fighting here—it's just grace" (Kurdzeil).

But even in a community like the Crossing, where reaching "the other" has been a core value from the start, radical welcome is always a work in progress. Kurdzeil notes that she and her wife will likely soon become parents. "I don't know that Thursday 6 p.m. worship is going to fit our lifestyle anymore," she said. "Does radical welcome apply to families with young kids—and should it? We can't be everything to everyone" (Kurdzeil).

Communion and Community

Thirty to forty people gather around the cathedral's altar for Crossing worship. The altar and keyboard are draped in colorful fabric, with candles and hanging lamps enhancing the sense of intimacy and mystery. Several stations are available for "open-space time" after the homily—meditation with an icon, anointing and healing prayer, or discussion of the homily. The Prayers of the People are the worshipers' own petitions and intercessions. As Everett explained, "The Crossing would rather have D+ prayers written by someone we know and love, rather than A+ prayers we got off the internet. There's real value in 'buying local'—contributing to the local spiritual economy" (Everett, Personal interview 1). Similarly, the presider improvises the Eucharistic prayer.

Music also sets this liturgy apart from inherited forms, including congregational chant of the Gospel reading. The instrumentation and arrangements are jazzy, but more significant is the sense of music as a soundtrack to the worship. Improvised instrumental music runs under most of the liturgy in order to connect with

Millennials' ears: "A traditional worship service is structured like a Broadway musical," Everett said. "You've got dialogue, and you stop the dialogue for a song; then more dialogue and another song." He argues that's not the genre of most Millennials. "We grew up on film, and the language of film is very different. There's an undercurrent, an underscoring of music" (Everett, Personal interview 2).

After Holy Communion comes more communion, with the worshipers adjourning to a local Mexican restaurant to continue the fellowship and theological reflection. "The fajitas and margaritas are just as much Communion for us as the bread and wine," said Crossing treasurer (and non-Episcopalian) Shane Montoya (Montoya).

Crossing and Cathedral: An Organizational Dance

Birthed in 2005, the Crossing is one of the longest-lived new expressions of church rising out of Episcopal congregations. In that time, the Crossing and St. Paul's have plowed new ground in this kind of not-quite-church-planting, and they've created a structure for something approaching autonomy in the Crossing's life.

During Spellers's time, the Crossing had no elected board or governing body, and a diocesan fellowship paid Spellers's salary for its first few years. When that fellowship ran out, Spellers remained with the Crossing, raising most of the community's funding (including her pay). "That was the beginning of their independence," Streit said. "Most of their money came from beyond the cathedral, so it wasn't like I could say, 'Do this' or 'Do that.' The community made decisions largely by consensus" (Streit, Personal interview 2).

By the spring of 2010, the Crossing formed three "circles" to oversee worship, the community's life, and mission. Each circle had two conveners, and those conveners came together monthly "for big-picture conversations, like a vestry would," Everett explained—but all the meetings began to burn out the leaders (Everett, Personal interview 1). Once Spellers left in August 2012 and the community was overseen by an interim priest, the Crossing needed more explicit organization and lines of accountability. "But it was problematic," Streit said. "They didn't want to be a hierarchical community. They didn't want to be run by a governing board. They wanted to be consensual, peer-led, and decentralized. So they sort of felt their way" to developing a subsidiary governing body—the Council (Streit, Personal interview 2).

Created in 2013, the Council deals with finance, leadership, and vision. It includes two paid staff members, two elected Crossing members, an elected treasurer, and representatives from the two remaining circles, worship and mission ("Council"). Specifically, the Council creates and implements an annual budget, oversees fundraising, maintains relationships with the cathedral and diocese, makes personnel recommendations to the cathedral dean and chapter, and oversees the work of all Crossing committees and teams (Crossing Leadership Structure Task Force).

Not surprisingly, most of the Council's interaction with the cathedral chapter (leadership body) has been about money. In 2012, when Spellers left, the Crossing ended the year with its first deficit. The Crossing's treasurer began meeting with the cathedral's budget and finance committee, which offered coaching rather than criticism—a relationship of grace. "When there were deficits, we covered them because the Crossing has been a program of the Cathedral," Streit said. "We give them money and expect them to meet the budget; but if they don't, we're not going to hang them out to dry" (Streit, Personal interview 2).

The 2012 deficit spurred Crossing leaders to tend the relationship with the cathedral more intentionally. "The Crossing still wants to know it can make its own decisions, and the Crossing does feel it's responsible for making its own money," Everett said. "But locating ourselves within the wider constellation of the cathedral congregations is more important now because we realize how much we benefit from that relationship, and they benefit from their relationship with us" (Everett, Personal interview 1).

But for a new expression of church that deeply values its independence, the dance of autonomy-in-community is tricky. "The question is: How do we fit into the bigger picture?" said Council member Kurdzeil. "As a community, we really are not the cathedral. We're separate entities." She describes the Crossing and the cathedral as different parts of an extended family. "We're like the cousins who live off on this farm doing really cool things and rejecting the city folk. But the city folk are like, 'I'd really love to come to the farm, if you'd invite me.' And vice versa. We'd probably love going to the city if we felt like we could be comfortable. But we don't necessarily have that relationship yet" (Kurdzeil).

ST. JOHN'S CATHEDRAL AND THE WILDERNESS, DENVER

The Cathedral of St. John in the Wilderness breaks open boundaries between heaven and earth for all sorts and conditions of people in downtown Denver's Capitol Hill. The cathedral's neighborhood includes gentrified, million-dollar homes; camps of homeless people on the cathedral's grounds; head shops, clubs, and marijuana boutiques; the state capitol with its legislators and staffers; and my personal favorite, just down the street from the offices of the Diocese of Colorado, a Goth clothing and accessories shop called Baby Sitter's Nightmare. (At least it was there when I visited.) For any or all of these neighbors, the cathedral's primary connecting point is its stunning worship.

Glory in the Wilderness

The cathedral features three auditioned adult choirs, as well as four boys' and girls' choirs in a program affiliated with the Royal School of Church Music in America ("St. John's Cathedral Choir School"). Annually, St. John's offers more than 200 services with musical support, including monthly evensongs and concerts during the school year ("Liturgical Music"). Visually, the cathedral's glorious windows lift the worshiper's eye heavenward. The intent of the designer of several of its stained-glass windows, Charles Connick, applies to all the cathedral's art: "I want to make beautiful interiors for both churches and souls," Connick wrote. "I want people to hear my windows singing" (A. L. Jones 22).

The artistic opulence complements the cathedral's Sunday morning worship, which features Sanctus bells, incense-led processions, and a chanted Gospel proclamation. The connection with traditional Anglo-Catholic worship is almost literally concrete: When St. John's burned in 1903, the cathedral chose an old-world Gothic design, with vaulted ceilings, towering windows, and foundation stones brought from Westminster Abbey and Canterbury Cathedral (St. John's Cathedral). But treasuring tradition doesn't keep St. John's from breaking down liturgical boundaries. At the midmorning Sunday service, children and youth serve as ushers and greeters, and kids gather around the altar on the chancel steps for the Eucharistic prayer.

In 2007, cathedral leaders began developing alternative worship for neighbors who weren't coming Sunday mornings. Some cathedral staff wanted a liturgy influenced by emergent church styles; some simply wanted to offer a quick evening service for hikers and skiers. "I thought this was going to be a pick-up mass for twenty-five people who couldn't be there on Sunday morning, and I'd have been happy with just that," said the Rt. Rev. Peter Eaton, dean of St. John's from 2002 to 2015 and now bishop of the Diocese of Southeast Florida (P. Eaton).

As cathedral staff and Kate Eaton—a musician, composer, and the dean's spouse—began planning the new service, they hoped to attract unchurched and de-churched neighbors, especially Millennials. "We wanted to pull in some of the twenties and thirties, ragtag, tattooed, kind of angry, Goth-looking crowd that was around us," Kate Eaton said—though the planning team didn't include any of those neighbors (K. Eaton, Personal interview 1).

What evolved was both a new liturgy—the Wilderness, Sundays at 6 p.m.—and a new process for worship design, created by Kate Eaton. Other congregations now use that process to discern the shape of alternative worship for their contexts, launch new services, and then sustain the effort. The result, Mishkhah, is intended to be "worship grounded in the beauty and wonder of the tradition, sacraments, and architecture of Anglicanism" involving "careful integration of music, images, textures, found objects, light, movement, and prayer," according to Kate Eaton's website (K. Eaton, "Services").

Wilderness worship is Eucharist designed around a series of four- to eight-week "seasons" tying into the church year. Each season has its own musical style and thematic focus. Across its seasons, Wilderness worship features world music that's hard to describe—worshipers call it ambient, primal, cross-cultural, rhythmic, cinematic, tribal, exotic, joyful, and dissonant with church. "I feel like I could be sitting in an old holy land, in a temple," said Wilderness worshiper Missy Bell. "I could be sitting in Mombasa, on a street corner, hearing the same rhythms. I could be in Brazil and dancing in Carnival and hear the same threads running through it" (Bell). Many of the pieces are traditional hymns rearranged in nontraditional ways by the Wilderness band—four professional musicians who sing and play piano, electric keyboards, percussion, and string instruments reflecting the culture the music is seeking to evoke (a balalaika, for example).

The music is a strong differentiator, said the Rev. Canon Jadon Hartsuff, who now oversees the Wilderness: "If we didn't do anything else but have a dark cathedral and that band playing their music, everybody would walk in and say, 'Yeah, that's the Wilderness'" (Hartsuff, Personal interview 1). That identity doesn't come cheap. The Wilderness band costs $400 a week, but Peter Eaton believes it's vital: "This is not an opportunity for Uncle Joe and Cousin Sam to bring their banjos on a Sunday evening and play hymns," he said. "If this is going to be serious worship, it should be serious like the morning worship—professionally done, with professional musicians" (P. Eaton). Added Kate Eaton: "We'd rather not do this if it's schlocky" (K. Eaton, Personal interview 2).

Also central to the Wilderness experience are the individual prayer stations that worshipers visit during the liturgy's open-space time (which serves as Prayers of the People). At the high altar, with candles burning and illuminated smoke rising from an incense burner, worshipers can sit on the floor to meditate with icons. They can light candles or color mandalas. Colored fabrics drape the stations, and lighting casts evocative shadows on the wall. The ten-minute contemplative time is deeply connective for worshiper

Georgann "Bunny" Low. "It's about awareness of divine reality," she said. "This service opens a door to the presence of God that traditional liturgy doesn't. Traditional liturgy is so much talking. You need the quiet to feel the presence in this sacred space" (Low).

In the Wilderness's first two and a half years, when Kate Eaton led worship design and set-up, the prayer stations were nearly works of art themselves. "When Kate did them, they were beautiful and elaborate," Hartsuff said. "There were fabrics and special paper and oils with every kind of scent" (Hartsuff, Personal interview 2). With Eaton's departure, the complexity and variety was hard for the liturgy team to sustain. "When Kate was there, you walked into that service, and it blew your mind," said parishioner Priscilla Shand, part of the set-up team. "Little did I know the three hours it took to set it up. Since then, we've simplified it. But some people miss the 'Ta da!'" (Shand).

Who's It For?

The Wilderness uses its alternative worship to reach those whom inherited worship doesn't reach. In breaking down boundaries this way, St. John's took a more traditional approach compared with the Crossing in Boston. At the Crossing, the model was to organize a community and see how worship, fellowship, and mission might grow from it. At the Wilderness, the model was to organize worship and see how community might grow among the people who came.

But who is the intended audience? Hikers, skiers, and people who work Sunday mornings? Millennials? Goths? Yuppies? Any or all of the above? When the Wilderness began, St. John's staff and parishioners weren't exactly sure; and they still don't have a specific group in mind beyond unchurched and de-churched people. As worship planners create one season after another, "Hopefully, the conversation is representative of the wider community, asking some of the questions the unchurched folks would ask," Kate Eaton said (K. Eaton, Personal interview 1).

But who *aren't* being attracted in large numbers are those elusive Millennials. Of the eighty or so people attending the

Wilderness, typically less than a quarter are in their twenties and thirties. To Hartsuff, himself a Millennial, it's no surprise: "Everybody thinks we should be doing something to attract the twenty-five-year-olds, when in reality most of the fresh expressions that I've seen, and certainly the Wilderness, are designed by fifty-year-old women for fifty-year-old women and attract and nurture fifty-year-old women," he said. "If fifty-year-old women need a fresh expression, let's provide them with a fresh expression. But let's stop pretending that we're doing this to draw in the twenties and thirties crowd, because in fact they're looking for something very different. They're actually looking for more tradition, not less" (Hartsuff, Personal interview 1).

Community? Commitment?

Another part of the Wilderness's model is to encourage anonymity—for good and perhaps for ill. The worshipers "want to be anonymous, and they're there because they can be," Peter Eaton said. "They're not interested in telling me why they're there or in coming to much of anything else" (P. Eaton). St. John's doesn't apologize that people slip in and out without being asked to make a commitment. Bell, a cathedral and Wilderness worshiper, sees the anonymity as a blessing because it attracts people who wouldn't come otherwise. "Their faces might be red from crying, but they're really getting something that I don't see on the faces of the people on Sunday mornings," she said (Bell). Clergy have tried to build community around worship; for years, Wilderness attendees were invited to a local bar, the Cheeky Monk, for drinks and conversation afterward. But the gathering was usually five to twelve of the eighty-person congregation. Now the cathedral is offering dinner and a class after the Wilderness, with fifteen to twenty people attending.

Although anonymity is a draw, it raises questions about membership and stewardship. It's a tension other congregations are also experiencing: Will people in new ministries join the congregation and fill out pledge cards? And if not, are the new ministries sustainable? What's the return on the congregation's investment?

Peter Eaton believes Sunday morning members shouldn't expect Wilderness worshipers to approach church like they do. Wilderness worshipers "aren't going to give like the morning crowd gives," he said. "They're not going to participate like the morning crowd participates; they're not going to submit to activities like formation and outreach like the morning crowd will. They're not interested in having ownership of the Wilderness. They don't even know what that means—and if they knew, they'd leave" (P. Eaton). Larry Kueter, a recent cathedral senior warden, says connecting with the downtown community is simply part of St. John's mission. "The Wilderness feels like something we should be doing," Kueter said. "You hope there's a membership benefit from that, but it wasn't done on a return-on-investment basis" (Kueter).

Boundaries Inside: Is the Wilderness in the Wilderness?

Cathedral leaders have always sought to protect Wilderness worshipers from too much connection with the larger cathedral community. "One of the hardest things for me as dean was to keep the churched at the cathedral from trying to church the Wilderness," Peter Eaton said. "A lot of the morning people are there because they love running the church. But for the Wilderness people, that's not where they are" (P. Eaton). Hartsuff agrees: "Originally there was a sense that the Wilderness might be sabotaged by forces of the cathedral if it wasn't intentionally very, very separate" (Hartsuff, Personal interview 1).

Cathedral leaders say it's hard to find the right relationship between inherited church and this new expression. For example, Peter Eaton believes the cathedral shouldn't ask Wilderness worshipers to participate in pledge campaigns because doing so reinforces negative attitudes about the church always asking for money. Kueter agrees stewardship in the Wilderness should be different from what happens Sunday morning. For the Wilderness, he says, "First, ask them to come regularly and keep coming. Second, ask them to participate—consider helping with the service or some other cathedral ministry. Third, remind them that, if you're so inclined and can pledge, that's appreciated—but with a more subtle message than we give the rest of the congregation" (Kueter).

Parishioners also note the balancing act between connection and differentiation. Bell describes the Wilderness's life as "carved out" from the larger cathedral, and she says the unchurched and de-churched people there likely don't consider themselves cathedral members. The Wilderness's representation among cathedral leadership also seems to be a work in progress. Vestry member Suni Devitt is a Wilderness regular who campaigned several years before winning a vestry seat. Now she unofficially brings a voice from the Wilderness to the table. "It's been good for somebody from the Wilderness to be part of the vestry, hear what's going on, and be an advocate for the service," she said, "because I think there are folks who feel like the Wilderness is a little bit of a step-child, not the same" as Sunday morning (Devitt).

Boundaries Outside: Wrestling with Welcome

The Wilderness's anonymity and transcendent worship clearly meet a need for cathedral neighbors, including homeless people. Like many congregations, the cathedral is wrestling with what it means to be a "neighbor" in the community where God has placed it. The night I visited the Wilderness, seventeen people stayed after worship for the dinner and a study with Peter Eaton. The seventeen included six men who appeared to be living on the street. They sat at tables apart from the other eleven diners. During the class time, it was the apparently homeless men who most often responded to Eaton's questions and seemed most engaged in the material.

Wilderness worshiper Bell admits concerns about the experience: "I have to tell you: It's hard to stay because of that. I'd rather go home and relax and not sit next to someone who hasn't bathed in a week and chews with his mouth open and smells like he's been drinking all day." Like many parents with school-aged kids, Bell wants the family to relax on Sunday nights. "We run crazy all week long with soccer and cross country, and we just want to sit and have a nice family dinner on Sundays," she explained. After Wilderness worship, "We want to stay and get our Sunday school time. But when there are only fifteen people there and six of them are off the street . . ." (Bell).

Yet even this huge boundary is slowly breaking down at St. John's. Shand notes that the most recent edition of the cathedral's pictorial directory includes a handful of photos she would never have seen before. In the directory, "there are probably six to eight homeless people who I recognize from the Wilderness," she said. "I just love that. I don't know that you'd ever see them in big church, but I see them very regularly—more regularly than a lot of other people—at the Wilderness. They're there every week. We are their home" (Shand).

ST. ANDREW AND ALL SOULS, PORTLAND, OREGON

Standing on the corner occupied by St. Andrew and All Souls in Portland, Oregon, the out-of-towner wonders: Where are the coffeehouses and food trucks? Apparently not every part of Portland is *Portlandia*—especially not the working-class northern neighborhoods people call the city's "fifth quadrant." It's not a great sign, being nicknamed as an afterthought.

St. Andrew's has ministered to the Portsmouth and St. John's neighborhoods in the heart of north Portland since 1895. But by 2012, the congregation had dwindled to eighteen people on a Sunday, singing along with a parishioner and his accordion in a 1950s A-frame designed for about 150. It wasn't sustainable.

A Marriage of Kingdom Convenience

At the same time, a spiritual entrepreneur had come to Portland looking for her next gig. The Rev. Karen Ward rose to prominence in Episcopal, Lutheran, and emerging church circles for creating Church of the Apostles (COTA) and the Fremont Abbey in Seattle. She started COTA in 2002 as a joint Lutheran-Episcopal ministry, and it became one of the mainline's most successful examples of emerging church. COTA was known for gathering Millennials through worship that's "postmodern but premodern at the same time," Ward said, following the ancient shape of the Eucharistic liturgy; embracing inherited liturgical elements like candles, incense, and chant; and gathering in a setting more like a living room than a pew-filled church (Ward, Personal interview 1). Local performers created new worship music that resonated with Millennials' tastes. Worshipers sat on couches or on the floor. Projections on the walls illustrated scriptural themes and led people through worship without books or bulletins. COTA members also were invited to adopt a rule of life integrating work, prayer, and rest; and COTA connected with its neighborhood through the arts ministries of its Fremont Abbey. COTA and the Abbey translated Benedictine spirituality and a deeply sacramental worldview into a fresh expression of church that many in The Episcopal Church have wanted to emulate.

But by 2012, Ward said, she felt called to move on from her work in Seattle, so she came to a new place of "cultural ferment" to plant an emerging expression: Portland. After consulting with a parish for a few months, Ward started building community in coffeehouses and bars, bringing like-hearted spiritual explorers together—people in their twenties and thirties, many of them gay or lesbian, all of them distant from inherited expressions of church. She offered a moveable Wednesday night prayer group, "Pop-Up Church," for a few months and gathered a community of about fifteen. All this was on her own initiative. "I didn't have a job; I didn't talk to the bishop," Ward said. "I usually don't ask for permission first. I just kind of do things" (Ward, Personal interview 1).

Ward convinced the bishop of Oregon to sanction her pop-up gatherings as a new Eucharistic community. But as the group was about to sign a lease on worship space, the bishop came back with a counteroffer: Bring her emerging community together with the faithful remnant that was St. Andrew's. It wasn't exactly what Ward had in mind, but "that's kind of how the Spirit works," she said. So the eighteen remaining members of St. Andrew's and about ten members of Ward's new community came together in late

2012 to form St. Andrew and All Souls (SAAS). "We just kind of looked at each other and said, 'What are we going to do?' So that's what we started with—an instant intergenerational church," Ward said (Ward, Personal interview 1). Today, that community understands itself much more specifically—a "catholic, evangelical, and progressive" Episcopal congregation, "informed by monastic practice in the Benedictine tradition" of prayer and work—or, as SAAS names it, worship and service ("FAQ").

Worship: Inherited, Emerging, Blended

Ward immediately faced another unexpected twist: SAAS would begin with two Sunday morning services—inherited *and* emerging expressions of Eucharist. The governing board wrote it into Ward's letter of agreement. Left to her own devices, she would never have begun that way; she says best practice in church redevelopment is to bring one service to critical mass (75 percent of sanctuary capacity) before starting new worship. But "doing two tracks from day 1 was necessary to seal the 'merger,'" Ward said, "so the remnant congregation would accept me and the ten All Souls' folk. The traditional liturgy was like an insurance policy to the remnant that their traditions would not be erased" (Ward, E-mail).

Both the inherited and emerging expressions drew in newcomers, with the inherited service growing by about 50 percent and the emerging liturgy almost doubling. Membership is about seventy now. But offering two services was "an overreach," Ward said, because of the cost involved to hire quality musicians to play two different genres (Ward, E-mail). Again, the parish found itself with an unsustainable model.

Meanwhile, after about a year of trust-building and fellowship among the elders and newcomers, several longtime members asked for a monthly blended service, integrating the inherited liturgy with emerging forms. Finally, in late 2014, SAAS moved to a single blended service each week—Ward's preference from the beginning. Connection-building between elders and newcomers ("coffee-cup diplomacy," Ward said), coupled with a fiscal crisis, spurred the shift. Needing to trim expenses, "the first thing folks said was, 'Let's ditch doing two services,'" Ward explained. "So, we're back to my original vision but by a long, hard, and winding road" (Ward, E-mail).

Eventually, Ward intends to move back to the two-service model to serve a broader spectrum of north Portland residents. But when that happens depends on money, as well as growth.

Feeding, Clothing, Arts—Yesterday and Today

SAAS is blessed with a large property and a long history of using it to reach people nearby. Below the worship space is a generous undercroft, which for three decades has housed a community theater group. Just to the north is the original church building now used as a pantry offering food, clothing, and household items. To the south is a former neighborhood library now owned by the church. SAAS has used the building as a senior center and a thrift store, a community connection that also brought in a few dollars to support the pantry.

All this space is both a rich resource for mission and an ongoing source of conflict. The theater group still uses the church basement, but the relationship has become complicated. Ward wants to create an interdisciplinary arts center, something like Fremont Abbey in Seattle, using the undercroft for concerts, poetry readings, and films. But some longtime parishioners hear plans for expansion as a way to end the old theater group, which a parishioner began thirty years ago. "I'm not trying to kick them out," Ward said. "But we'll have to change how we operate with them. They're going to have to learn how to play in a sandbox that has other people in it" (Ward, Personal interview 2).

The food pantry is another example of conflict in change. The pantry serves about four hundred people over three days a week. Longer-term members of SAAS are proud of the effort; former junior warden Nathan Keith says the pantry's director "needs to be put up for sainthood" (Keith). But newer SAAS members argue the operation doesn't achieve its potential, duplicates other nearby services, and doesn't welcome their input. Ward wants to turn the pantry building into a neighborhood social-services center, offering counseling, nurse visits, and dental services, as well as distributing food and household items. She says her model would generate about $1,000 per month from renting office space to counselors, as well as improving community health. But as with the theater group, some longer-term parishioners hear plans for change as a way to kill the traditional ministry. "We're not at all trying to shut down the pantry," Ward says. "We want it to grow and expand. But we also want it to be efficient, and we want the building to be viable financially. That means some changes in how you do things" (Ward, Personal interview 2).

The narrative of mission intertwined with conflict continues with the old library building. When Ward arrived, the thrift shop was open only four days a month and was serving few neighborhood residents. That, plus a conflicted relationship with a former parishioner who was still running the thrift shop, prompted the bishop to close it. The building is in a great commercial location, on the neighborhood's main drag—and remarkably, there's not a coffeehouse in sight. Ward wants to open a nonprofit coffeehouse and art space in the old library building, a place where SAAS can live out a Eucharistic ethos of feeding and welcoming every day. The coffeehouse would help fund the church's social-service work, the multidisciplinary arts program, and other neighborhood charities. "Because it's nonprofit, people would have a reason to come," Ward says. "Neighbors would know they're supporting the food pantry, helping the poor—so it's a social enterprise" (Ward, Personal interview 2).

What happens to the old library building will say much about the future of SAAS. If the coffeehouse vision becomes reality, "it can be part of the solution for the long-term viability" of SAAS ministries, Ward said, as well as opening a new welcoming door for people who don't see church as a place to find community (Ward, Personal interview 2). Said Keith, the former junior warden: "We have that asset of the building on the corner. What we do with it may leave us defined as we are, or it could change our definition of St. Andrew's" (Keith). It's a powerful instrument for breaking down boundaries, taking core values like feeding and welcoming out of the sanctuary and into day-to-day community interaction.

Who Is the Parish?

Changing the definition of St. Andrew's is on Ward's mind, too. What is the parish? Two congregations learning to cohabit the same property? Two subgroups learning to be one congregation? Or is the parish the "fifth quadrant" of Portland?

Members of SAAS, both newer and longer term, agree they've moved beyond cohabitation to become a single congregation. "It's more like old guard and new guard," says Justin Morgan, a newer member and writer of the beautiful icons that now adorn SAAS's worship space. The long-term members "who stuck around were aware of what's going on, and they decided to connect with it. That prevented it from being two different congregations" (Morgan). Keith agrees, arguing the common call to serve the community is what binds the two subgroups together. "Worship has changed some; the mission hasn't," he said. "I think if you get people bought into the mission, the rest of it doesn't matter so much. I can live with some candles or incense or whatever" (Keith).

But for Ward, unity is only one step in a larger movement to define the parish more broadly and push the congregation past its boundaries. She sees the parish geographically, the eleven neighborhoods of the richly diverse "fifth quadrant." That perspective both spurs the call to mission and fights the temptation to see the parish as something existing members own. "My view is there's 50,000 in our parish," Ward said. And part of the point of the community arts ministry is to build community members' investment in SAAS, seeing it as theirs regardless of whether they worship at the church. To break down the boundary of members' parochialism and sense of ownership of "their" church, Ward says they have to experience the people around them. "That's why I'm trying to get our people to come to these arts events," Ward says. "It takes a lot of experience with 'them' to move past the mindset of 'my' church" (Ward, Personal interview 2).

Faithful Practice Is Mission

For Ward, reaching that parish of 50,000 isn't a matter of marketing or even door-to-door proclamation. She turns the model around, focusing on who's really responsible for changing hearts through Good News. "We are trying to be the Church, and as we do, some people will notice that," Ward explained. "It's not promotion. We're being authentic and living with integrity, and that's the most important way to reach people. It's our job to be Christians in the world, and evangelism is the job of the Holy Spirit. So we do our job, and the Holy Spirit will do the Holy Spirit's job" (Ward, Personal interview 1).

Ward is intentional about forming people into "Christians in the world." A Benedictine ethos of work and prayer, captured in a rule of life, guides the congregation's discipleship, forming a community that practices Eucharist in everything it does. Ward sees Eucharist in the congregation's food pantry, arts ministries, neighborhood coffeehouse, *and* worship—all ways to welcome God's people, feed physical and spiritual hunger, and build community. "In every one of our buildings, Eucharist and hospitality will be available," Ward said. "We want to serve all the people of the neighborhood in some form; so our different enterprises allow us to touch lots of different people, regardless of their religious affiliation—or not" (Ward, Personal interview 1).

All of this is no accident. Ward came with the end in mind—a vision of Benedictine practice already working at COTA in Seattle. "I put out my vision for the whole church—how we're going to run things, what's the theology behind it all. I set that out for them, the leaders approved it unanimously, and I haven't deviated from it one iota," Ward said (Ward, Personal interview 2).

That vision has now become a congregational rule of life, a set of spiritual practices centered on the "postures" of radical welcoming, listening, receiving, practicing, participating, and inviting. "I know exactly what I'm doing." Ward said. "I operate off this vision, I keep reminding the people of it, and the rule of life makes it real for people" (Ward, Personal interview 2).

Living that kind of life, congregations can break down boundaries between church and community one loving, hospitable, Eucharistic act at a time. "It takes cultivating a certain kind of spirituality in people," Ward explained. "I didn't grow up with poor people; my parents sent me to private schools. So it's not my background, but I'm learning to expand my horizons. We've got to get rid of 'us' and 'them'—because 'they' *are* us" (Ward, Personal interview 2).

St. Paul's and the 5 p.m. Community, Seattle

The Pacific Northwest consistently leads the nation in its proportion of unchurched and de-churched people. New expressions like Church of the Apostles (COTA) in Seattle have succeeded in translating ancient liturgical and spiritual practices into a haven for spiritually hungry Millennials and Gen Xers. But what about congregations with a long history of inherited church? Anglo-Catholic St. Paul's Episcopal Church in Seattle, founded in 1892, is expanding its boundaries of Anglo-Catholic worship and Benedictine spirituality, using its identity as a stage on which to improvise with the Holy Spirit in reaching people longing for the paradoxically structured freedom of Anglican worship and community.

Roots: Location and Identity

Beginning as a log cabin mission, St. Paul's bought property in the Queen Anne neighborhood north of downtown Seattle in 1903. In the late 1950s, the parish bought new property "up the hill" in the area's affluent, growing residential section. But a new rector and a change of missional heart led St. Paul's to sell off its new property and double down on its location closer to the city center. It built a new worship space as part of the area's revitalization leading up to the 1962 World's Fair, and it's been there ever since ("Parish History").

Along with its location, St. Paul's is deeply rooted in its progressive and Anglo-Catholic identity. St. Paul's led Seattle churches in its pastoral response to the AIDS epidemic of the 1980s, opening its doors for memorial services for AIDS victims. In the 1990s, the parish called a partnered gay priest as rector ("Parish History"). Along with its welcome of the LGBTQ community, St. Paul's continued to cultivate its Anglo-Catholic and Benedictine sensibility—emphasizing sacramental life, honoring the holiness of creation and embodiment, practicing daily corporate prayer, and engaging a spiritual life of wonder and adoration. Its elegant liturgies regularly include incense, chanting, Sanctus bells, rich vesture, and veneration of saints ("Anglo-Catholic").

But St. Paul's also hears God's call to take its sacramental identity beyond the boundaries of its sacred space—even literally. A 2011 renovation included a new baptismal font (complete with living water) in the entryway, as well as redesigning the walls and doors to be glass. That way, passersby on busy Roy Street can look in and see the core of Christian identity—dying and rising with Christ. When someone is baptized—by partial immersion, with the candidate kneeling before the font—baptismal water spills out onto the floor, running out the front door and onto the sidewalk, sharing the water of life with all who walk by.

Managing and Building Growth

A watershed moment in St. Paul's life came in 2005, when it called as rector the now Rt. Rev. Melissa Skelton (currently bishop of New Westminster in the Anglican Church of Canada). It was significant not just because Skelton was St. Paul's first female rector but because of her focus on congregational growth. When she arrived, about 90 people worshiped at St. Paul's on a Sunday; now, Sunday attendance is about 250. The growth began quickly, Skelton said, and soon the principal service had reached about 80 percent of capacity. Skelton knew it was time to add another liturgy—but what kind, and at what time? She taught the congregation about growth patterns and how a full worship space can make growth plateau. From parish meetings, Skelton heard interest in starting an evening service, which was her preference, too. She didn't want to weaken what was happening on Sunday mornings "because what we were offering had game," she explained. "We needed to create something new that was connected to the identity but was not identical to what we were doing Sunday morning" (Skelton).

To design a new liturgy, Skelton created a discernment group that included not just parish leaders but people representing

populations St. Paul's hoped the new liturgy would reach—
lapsed Roman Catholics, LGBTQ seekers, and young adults
"burned out on evangelical or charismatic Protestantism," said
Mark Taylor, St. Paul's senior warden, a professor of theology at
Seattle University, and a member of the discernment group (M.
Taylor). In fact, the liturgy has drawn people from all of those
groups, especially the third.

Skelton sees each parish liturgy as a distinct worshiping community, not simply different scheduling options. So, about a year
after the 5 p.m. service began, Skelton delegated some of its pastoral oversight to a "worship community developer"—someone
tasked with turning the new service into "the 5 p.m. Community."
For each of St. Paul's liturgies, a parishioner is empowered to be a
"minirector," Skelton said, overseeing liturgical preparation, offering hospitality afterward, making announcements, and leading
newcomer follow-up. But for the new 5 p.m. liturgy, that role went
to the next level, a lay pastor. Paul Steinke started as community
developer in 2006, coming from the Seattle School of Theology
and Psychology, where he now serves as vice president of student
and alumni development. Skelton hadn't planned to give Steinke
greater leadership, but "his community and connections began
to represent a pretty large group of the people who came," she
said. "They were young evangelicals seeking a way back into the
church and seeking a dialogical, improvisational, but ordered way
of liturgical life" (Skelton).

Building a Worshiping Community

With Steinke on board, the proportion of former charismatics
and evangelicals at 5 p.m. began growing. About half the community now comes from that background. Steinke says they're
attracted by the beauty and order of Anglo-Catholic worship
and the rhythm of Benedictine prayer. But he also says they're
drawn by an Anglican focus on worship rather than specific
beliefs. "Doubt and faith, they're almost lovers," he explained.
"You need them both. But you don't get that in an evangelical
tradition based on belief. So part of what's helpful for former

charismatics and evangelicals is the very bodily emphasis of The Episcopal Church—that it's really about gathering around practice" (Steinke, Personal interview 2).

Building the community has happened the old-fashioned, apostolic way—one person and one relationship at a time. "We did some initial advertising, but then we just didn't," Skelton said. "Paul worked Facebook and his own personal relationships; I taught homiletics at the Seattle School; we engaged people when they came—all that helped build the community" (Skelton). Now, the 5 p.m. Community is about forty to fifty people, thirty to forty of whom come on any given Sunday (Steinke, Personal interview 2).

But, from an inherited-church perspective, are they members? Do they fill out pledge cards? Steinke argues membership is a decreasingly helpful concept, especially for Millennials. The 5 p.m. Community regularly sees young adults rotate in for a couple of years and rotate out again. "They don't want to be told how deeply to connect," Steinke said. "They might want to partner with you, but they're not necessarily going to join your party. If I'm expecting them to become lifelong Episcopal parishioners, well, that might be one out of fifty" (Steinke, Personal interview 2). Nevertheless, the 5 p.m. Community engages stewardship as a spiritual practice along with the rest of St. Paul's.

St. Paul's also bridges the 5 p.m. with the four other worship communities through its leadership bodies, festival worship, and fellowship. The vestry includes a 5 p.m. member, as did the profile and search committees during the 2014–2015 search for a new rector. St. Paul's gathers for common liturgies on major feasts, and parishioners have organized arts field trips to bring members of the different worship communities together. But Martin Pommerenke, a parishioner and parish administrator, notes that until 2014, St. Paul's database didn't necessarily include 5 p.m. Community members, which hampered parish-wide communication. "There are good things about being as decentralized as we are in this place," Pommerenke said, "but you also really have to reach out to the decentralized places and tease out information from them" (Pommerenke).

High-Church Improvisation

Even in a church basement—with worshipers seated around the altar in a flattened diamond shape, looking at each other—the vesture, icons, and incense let you know an Anglo-Catholic spirit empowers the 5 p.m. Community's liturgy. And yet, the experience is anything but a liturgical "fragile glass treasure people hope doesn't get dropped," as Taylor described stereotypical Anglo-Catholic worship (M. Taylor). Instead, it's become an experience of "improvisation within boundaries," Skelton said—like jazz in its collaborative freedom within order (Skelton).

The improvising began in the preaching. From the beginning, the liturgy's design team wanted to share preaching—not just including worshipers in the preaching rota but having each preaching moment be a collaborative experience. For about five minutes, the presider or lay pastor explores a theme from the readings, focusing on something fairly specific. Then the preacher hands off the ball, asking a question and inviting worshipers to offer their thoughts and experience. "It's like Godly Play," Steinke said. "I'll end my part of the sermon with, 'I wonder, what do you do with Jesus's statement here? I wonder whether or how it's true for you, in your life?' We've grown accustomed to saying, 'You had the homily tonight'—meaning someone just shared something, and that's the message." But there's no attempt at the end to tie up the homiletical package neatly with a bow (Steinke, Personal interview 2).

The improvisational spirit next entered into the 5 p.m. Community's music. Initially, Skelton said, the planning team designed the music to be similar to the experience of Sunday morning, though with slightly expanded hymnody. But soon "that felt too confining," she said. "We needed to go to something like jazz as a mirror of the improvisational nature of the homily" (Skelton).

Steinke says the musical style helps reach and form people coming from outside the boundaries of a typical Episcopal experience. "We began to wonder, 'How does jazz form us differently than the hymns we would do upstairs?' In jazz, there's a structure; people know the structure, and then they're able to improvise on it," Steinke said. That openness to improvisation allows people to feel part of worship in ways they've never experienced. "That's where it began—wanting to respond to a different generation, a younger generation, and some of the cultural movements occurring external to Christian culture in the Northwest" (Steinke, Personal interview 1). At this point, the musical mix is broad, drawing on hymns from the Episcopal, Lutheran, evangelical, and gospel traditions, improvised usually on piano.

The improvisational spirit even informs the Word itself. During the liturgical seasons and on feast days, the 5 p.m. Community experiences "an epistle" from an artist in residence, Steinke said (Steinke, Personal interview 2). Over several weeks, a poet, painter, dancer, or other artist will offer his or her work and reflect on it theologically—often grist for the mill of the shared homily. For example, on the first Sunday of Advent one year, a painter brought out a canvas with a work begun. After brief reflection, she invited worshipers to "make their mark" on the canvas, Skelton said. The artist progressed the work during the week, and the congregation added more of their own touches the next Sunday. "So it was an emerging, collective, artistic process," Skelton said. "In The Episcopal Church, and especially in the Anglo-Catholic tradition, beauty is the avenue to God. So we're always glimpsing the face of beauty as expressed in local artists and in the congregation" (Skelton). Karin Stevens—a parishioner, dancer, and one of the artists in residence—captures the connection this way: The artists offer "an embodied revealing of the divine" (Stevens).

"A Huge Sigh of Relief"

The 5 p.m. Community's high value of collaboration, improvisation, and aesthetics—its jazz spirituality—touches people whose experience of church hasn't affirmed the divine spark they bear. In this worshiping community, "we can encounter God in a way that is good and thoughtful, that happens in the moment, that happens in community," Pommerenke said. "And we can do this in an experience where anyone can walk in and enter something profound and elegant" (Pommerenke).

That was the story for parishioner Laura Griffin. She left her evangelical church because it didn't welcome her LGBTQ friends and because she found the worship overwhelming. "I was so burned out with the evangelical style—loud guitars and drums and raising of hands and all that," she said. "Coming to St. Paul's felt like a huge sigh of relief" (Griffin).

In the 5 p.m. Community, Griffin found not just embrace but an invitation to serve. She recently completed a term on the vestry, including a stint as junior warden, and she remains involved in St. Paul's stewardship ministries. Most important, she encountered the power of symbol and sacrament—and the freedom to construct meaning from that encounter on her own terms. "If somebody had tried to explain to me, 'This is why we use incense,' it would have felt very intellectual," she said. "I wouldn't have connected to it in the way that I do just experiencing it—seeing it, smelling it, swinging the thurible myself" (Griffin).

TEWKESBURY ABBEY, ENGLAND, AND CELEBRATE!

Tewkesbury Abbey—officially the parish church of St. Mary the Virgin in Tewkesbury, England—watches over its town like a loving but reserved mother, present and distant simultaneously. With its twisting alleys and streets lined with Tudor buildings, Tewkesbury may be the epitome of Cotswolds charm for the tourists. But the abbey has been the spiritual heart of this community for more than nine hundred years. In fact, when Henry VIII dissolved England's abbeys and seized church holdings, the people of Tewkesbury couldn't bear to see their abbey sold off and destroyed. Instead, residents petitioned to buy the abbey, paying Henry 453 pounds for the building. Today, the abbey still holds a beloved place in the hearts of the people around it, according to the Rev. Paul Williams, abbey vicar. "When I go out visiting, I find most houses will have a picture of the abbey up," he said. "It's their abbey, and they're very proud of it" (Williams).

At the same time, the abbey building isn't exactly warm and welcoming. At nearly 150 feet high, the twelfth-century tower dominates the landscape. Fourteen enormous columns march down the nave toward the altar, each more than 30 feet high and 6 feet thick. The effect is majestic—and a bit intimidating. "The building just mitigates against an immanent understanding of God," Williams said. "We can do transcendence by the bucketload, but we can't do immanence" (Williams). And so, authentic to that context, worship in the abbey is high "up the candle" of English churchmanship. The Sunday morning high mass features incense, Sanctus bells, and a chanted Gospel proclamation, the prayers of today's saints rising with those of the monks from centuries past.

The abbey's towering majesty and Anglo-Catholic worship draw 250,000 visitors every year but can act as a barrier for some of the people who live literally next door. Bordering the abbey's grounds is Prior's Park, a housing "estate" (public housing in England). The Park is part of the abbey's parish, but Park residents rarely venture into the abbey for anything other than baptisms, funerals, or an afternoon stroll. And many abbey worshipers typically keep their distance from the Park, too. Former parishioner Lara Bloom, now training for holy orders, describes the divide this way: "In the town, there's a perception that Prior's Park is a bit of a no-go area. When I first offered to help with ministry on Prior's Park, I wouldn't have driven my car through the estate" (Bloom). It's a place where poverty, substance abuse, dysfunctional relationships, and mental-health issues are part of day-to-day life.

Reaching Out by Moving In

The abbey has reached out in different ways to the approximately four thousand people in Prior's Park. The abbey had a chapel there, but it burned down about two decades ago and wasn't rebuilt. Typically, the abbey's curate (priest in training) served Park residents, though inexperience and the short-term curacy assignment made building deep connections difficult. "I always thought the Park deserved better than that," Williams said. "So I had this idea of having a pioneer minister build a church not *for* the community, but *with* the community. That word, 'with,' is really important" (Williams). (In the Church of England, pioneer ministry is a calling differentiated from inherited models of priesthood, though many pioneer ministers are priests.)

At the same time, in 2008, the now Rev. Wendy Ruffle came to Tewkesbury for a two-month posting as an ordinand in training. The Anglo-Catholic abbey was not exactly Ruffle's comfort zone. "I was a rampant charismatic evangelical when I came here to find out what on earth all this liturgical stuff was about," Ruffle said. "I said that to the teams at the abbey—that I don't get this stuff; I thought it was completely irrelevant, turgid, and boring for today's society. They kind of looked horror-struck at me." Ruffle raised the same issues with God, asking for some revelation about the Anglo-Catholic tradition. "My first Eucharist at the abbey, God went, wallop! I couldn't get up; the Lord had me held down on my knees. I was just weeping with what I'd experienced through receiving the bread and wine," she explained. "God totally transformed me in those eight weeks—and said to me, 'You're coming back'" (Ruffle, Personal interview 2).

Williams had the same idea. In Ruffle, he saw a pioneer minister who could build church with the people of Prior's Park from the bottom up. So he worked with church deployment officials to bring Ruffle to Tewkesbury for her curacy and create a new ministry on Prior's Park. Ruffle began what she imagined as a year-long process of "stretching myself into the community" to identify needs and gathering places, she said. The prime location was the local elementary school, and there the Holy Spirit chose an unlikely connecting point: table tennis. The school principal had just bought a table, though he didn't have a specific programmatic use in mind. "Well, I'm a table-tennis coach," Ruffle told him. So for years, she ran a table-tennis club in the school. "It showed them I was here for the long term and that it wasn't about Bible bashing," she said. "It's actually very incarnational, the work we're doing here—incarnating Christ" (Ruffle, Personal interview 1).

Ruffle's work at the school got her involved in the lives of Prior's Park residents and built trust. Although she expected to spend her first year in pioneer ministry simply getting to know the community and building relationships, she felt called to start a gathering for school families in December 2010, after only three months there. Similar to the English fresh expression model of "messy church," her gathering focused on kids' activities—crafts, games, puppetry, or drama—related to a theme from Scripture, as well as ten minutes of very light worship and a hot meal. For many of the people attending, it was their only hot meal of the day. "In everything we've done, I've had a real sense of the Lord saying, 'It needs to be extravagant in its blessing,'" Ruffle said. "The point is just to pour Christ's blessing over them" (Ruffle, Personal interview 1).

In November 2013, the new gathering was commissioned as a congregation in its own right, and Ruffle was named its vicar (she spends about 90 percent of her time working with people in Prior's Park and about 10 percent working at the abbey). By Easter 2014, the community's gatherings had grown into weekly Saturday afternoon worship—"Celebrate! The Abbey on the Park." It still follows the same basic model, with families coming together in the local school for an hour of crafts, games, or drama, followed by worship—now about forty-five minutes long and with Eucharist every six weeks or so—and a hot meal. Though it's very intentionally marketed as abbey worship, it follows Ruffle's charismatic evangelical heart, with easy-to-sing praise songs, kids waving "worship flags" on a stage, and a kid-friendly teaching time as the homily. The Celebrate! community numbers about fifty now, with thirty-five or so coming regularly for worship, Bible studies, moms' groups, and other activities.

"A Nice Warm Hug on a Rainy Day"

Nearly all those who come to Celebrate! are previously unchurched, never having experienced Christian community and knowing little of the abbey beyond architectural beauty and perceived social barriers. One young father in Celebrate!—struggling with addiction, depression, ADHD, a history of abuse, and only intermittent employment—described the contrast this way: "We're a different class, aren't we? You go into the abbey, and as soon as they look at your clothes, they're like, 'You come from Prior's Park.' Once they know where you live, that's it" (Celebrate! Planning Group). Ruffle described the experience of a young mom from the Park, who had gone to worship at the abbey for the first time: "Her body language was intense; she couldn't sit. She stood with her arms pinned against the pillar. This is how terrifying church is to some folk. Are they going to do the right thing or say the right thing? Are they going to be judged?" (Ruffle, Personal interview 2).

Overcoming those barriers meant making Celebrate! a contrast to the kind of church most Prior's Park residents had in mind. Worship still happens at the elementary school. It's very participatory, focused on images over words, with activities designed to bring kids and parents together. Although initial Celebrate! gatherings saw Ruffle and abbey volunteers putting on worship for the people of Prior's Park, she soon brought kids and parents into the action—singing, reading Scripture, playing parts in dramas. Before long, the sense of outside presentation gave way to collaborative, indigenous worship. "Some of the abbey team started to fall away, or be released, and members of the community stepped up and took their places," Bloom remembered. "As people got to know each other and trust was built in the community, segregating barriers were broken down, and there was much more mixing of people in worship" (Bloom).

The effect is a church community that images the immanent love of the family of God. After finding a Celebrate! flyer in her kids' schoolbook bags, one young mom came to Celebrate! and left transformed. "It just felt like a really happy, loving, safe place to be," she said. "I was somewhere I belonged—completely relaxed." Another mom described how Ruffle gave her a Bible and thereby brought her face-to-face with the divine: "God was trying to tell me, 'Yeah, I do still love you, even though you've strayed. You are loved, and I am your Father.' Walking into the school, it was like someone had wrapped a blanket around me. It's not something I experience very often. It was like someone giving you a nice warm hug on a rainy day" (Celebrate! Planning Group).

Though Ruffle invested herself deeply in Prior's Park from the beginning and was itinerate for three years, she now has her own missional base there: a vicarage, purchased with diocesan funds. The vicarage has become a gathering spot for Celebrate! members. Group meetings and parties happen there, as does the regular gathering of the leadership team—four or five parents who plan the weekly activity time, worship, and meal (prepared in the school kitchen by abbey volunteers). The parents could see that Ruffle was under pressure trying to organize the complex weekly gathering. "We went to Wendy and said, 'We need to make a group with us in it, so that we can help plan,'" said a Planning Group member. "Unbeknownst to us, Wendy had had the idea for a while, but she was waiting for us to be in the place where we would come to her with it" (Celebrate! Planning Group).

Ruffle believes both the abbey and Celebrate! must intentionally honor the connection they share. Celebrate! members often witness to the abbey congregation about the difference Celebrate! has made in their lives and their community. Parish-wide family activities around All Saints' and Easter bring Prior's Park residents and abbey worshipers together. "This is the abbey's parish [in a geographic sense]," she said. "Whilst Celebrate! is a fresh expression of church, it's very important that they know they are loved by their main church. We happen to meet in the school or in the vicarage on Prior's Park, but we're very much part of the abbey family" (Ruffle, Personal interview 2).

Minster and Mission

New expressions of church often embody an "ancient-future" outlook—rooted in Christian tradition, empowered by Scripture and sacrament, and sent to love God's world in the specific context of today. The irony is that Tewkesbury Abbey has been following that path for centuries. Building on what's gone before and taking the abbey to the Park is only the most recent example of what it means to be a "minster" church, raising up new expressions of Christian community in nearby areas. "This is exactly what the Benedictines did," Williams said. "The abbey was a minster. In Anglo-Saxon times, the abbey planted churches and resourced them all around this area. Actually, all we've done is rediscover the minster model" (Williams).

By building on its history, the abbey is figuring out how to be the church God is asking it to become in its next century and beyond. "If a church is caught in its past, it will die," Williams said. "So you have to honor the past and then try to take a prospective view on things, to look forward." But, Williams says, well-intentioned church planters must be careful not to take what's worked in a given context and try to transfer it into another. "Culture eats mission for breakfast," Williams explained, paraphrasing a well-known saying, "so you've got to get the culture right. That means being present, learning from the culture, not trying to go against it but using it" (Williams).

Celebrate! walks alongside the people it serves, blessing them by creating Christian community rooted in their own community and by connecting them with the image of God their lives and context demand. "The people of Prior's Park need a God that's beside them, whereas the abbey issues a picture of a God that's beyond them," Williams said. "They've got enough of that anyway—enough people beyond them, telling them what to do" (Williams).

St. Barnabas and Church@Five, London

A few blocks from the Woodside Park Tube station in north London, on a side street among lovely homes of physicians, attorneys, and business leaders, you find the parish church of St. Barnabas. Planted in 1886 and with a building dating from 1914 (though designed to hearken back at least a century earlier), St. Barnabas draws heavily from the affluent professionals in its neighborhood and beyond. But in London, you find social housing "estates" (public housing) in the midst of affluence, rich and poor living nearly side by side. The estates mark boundaries between wealth and poverty, but churches can be points of boundary crossing. "The rich and the poor don't mix except in church," said the Rev. Henry Kendal, St. Barnabas's vicar. "It's one of the wonders of the church, that you get rich people and poor people becoming friends, when they wouldn't anywhere else" (Kendal, Personal interview 2).

That works for poor people who live close by, including those who enjoy lunch at St. Barnabas after worship every Sunday. But for those beyond walking distance, the cost of public transport means life happens within a fairly small orbit. "It's hard for me to get to St. Barnabas—it's two bus rides and a walk, and I don't walk so well," said Josie Poulter, a resident of the Strawberry Vale housing estate two miles from St. Barnabas (Poulter). So, if they can't come to church, says St. Barnabas member Liz Kovar, "the church has to come to them" (Kovar). That's exactly what St. Barnabas has done with Church@Five, a fresh expression of church on Strawberry Vale.

And stepping into St. Barnabas, you're not a bit surprised. Being sent in mission is the lifeblood flowing through everything that happens there. High above the altar, juxtaposed with a lovely stained-glass window of Christ ascending in glory, is a huge poster. It looks like a stock photo decorating a big-box sporting-goods store. The image is a close-up of two feet—feet in running shoes, feet in mid-step, feet running away from you, feet sent somewhere beyond the boundaries they know.

Charismatic, Evangelical, Missional

The Episcopal Church prides itself on being a big tent, but the Anglican tent in England is even bigger. St. Barnabas is about as low "down the candle" of churchmanship as you can go. Its four Sunday services do include a spoken 8 a.m. Eucharist in a side chapel. But beyond that, its evangelical charismatic worship is much more like what you'd find in an American Vineyard congregation than in an Episcopal cathedral. A five-piece praise band rocks out on a stage under a large video screen, and video monitors hang from the pillars lining the nave. St. Barnabas offers Eucharist about once a month at its two main Sunday morning services. But even then, sacrament is but a prelude to Word, with a quick, improvised Eucharistic prayer setting the stage for the main work: the band's music, prayers for healing, words of prophesy, speaking in tongues, and a forty-minute sermon. St. Barnabas also offers a "more stripped-back, acoustic, church-in-the-round" service on Sunday evenings, said Sam Markey, one of the two church-wardens (senior lay leaders) (Markey). As St. Barnabas member Helen Davidson put it: "I was raised in the Church of England, but we had to go to St. Barnabas three times before we realized it was an Anglican church" (Davidson).

The iconography clearly communicates St. Barnabas's call to reach all sorts and conditions of people. Rather than featuring paintings or stations of the Cross, St. Barnabas's décor looks more like what you'd find in a corporate office, with posters outlining its vision, mission, and five-year goals and objectives. Alongside are displays about how to get involved in missional ministry, from sponsoring overseas missionaries to joining one of twelve "missional communities," groups building relationships and accountability while also focusing outward "on a local neighbourhood, a network, or a need in the community" ("Missional Communities"). "We are a church that is not interested in standing still," Kendal said. "We are passionate about mission, passionate about drawing people in from the fringes—not for them to come sit on their hands but to be released" (Kendal, Personal interview 2).

Sharing Our Lives Outrageously

The Rev. Helen Shannon is a case study in coming into St. Barnabas to be released. She has a bit of a "wayward" background, Shannon says, including being a single mom as a teenager. Her mother sent her to St. Barnabas, hoping she'd meet some "nice young people." There, Shannon experienced faith for the first time. "It wasn't that I didn't believe there was God," she said; "I just couldn't see how he was relevant to my life because I didn't know him." At St. Barnabas, people "allowed me, encouraged me, cajoled me to be the person God had created me to be," Shannon said. "They let me lead and start new ministries, and they didn't wait until I was squeaky clean" (Shannon, Personal interview 2).

Shannon began working at St. Barnabas as a custodian and eventually as a children's minister, offering programs for families from local housing estates. "We used to just bus them in," Shannon said. Her work led to a call to ordained ministry, specifically living in community with the poor. So, after training toward ordination, she was called back to St. Barnabas in 2008 to take up residence, with her husband and six children, on Strawberry Vale in a house St. Barnabas purchased (Shannon, Personal interview 2). The intent was not to plant a church but to form church from the bottom up. "We bought the house so she could live incarnationally on the estate, be part of them, form relationships," Kendal said. "Church@Five was spawned out of those relationships rather than being kind of a cold plant, being 'done unto' from people outside. It was very much Helen living alongside them, and this thing bubbled up from within" (Kendal, Personal interview 1).

The work began with Shannon and St. Barnabas volunteers simply connecting with people—"saying hello to everyone on the estate, getting into every conversation we could get in," she said. "We knew we wanted to build a worshiping community, but first and foremost we wanted to see God's kingdom come. We knew God was already there doing stuff; we needed to find what he was doing and join in with him." Shannon's team offered "prayer brunches," put postcards and candy through people's mail slots, and joined the team running Strawberry Vale's community center. The work was slow, pastoral, and deeply taxing. "Our door was constantly open, people constantly knocking. The calls, the texts—we were just right out there, all the time. We shared our lives with everybody in quite an outrageous way" (Shannon, Personal interview 1).

In 2010, Shannon began offering Sunday night worship in the Strawberry Vale community center—Church@Five. The shape of the worship is very similar to what happens on Sunday morning at St. Barnabas but emphasizes involvement rather than professional presentation. Estate residents co-officiate with Shannon, read Scripture, lead intercessions, serve Communion, offer healing prayer, and make announcements. A St. Barnabas minister leads a teaching sermon, but the proclamation is shared: Worshipers discuss Bible passages around tables as part of the sermon and share their conversations with the whole group. And worship always ends with a meal—eucharistic regardless of whether Eucharist is celebrated.

Since Shannon and her family came to live on Strawberry Vale, others have followed. St. Barnabas now has a core of about ten members and student ministers living in three units on the estate, as well as other visiting volunteers.

By building relationships, serving pastoral needs, and raising up people's participation in worship, Shannon sees Church@Five affirming the same truth St. Barnabas affirmed in her—that Strawberry Vale residents are made in the image and likeness of God. "Society says they're useless, that they can't do anything, that they haven't got any aspirations, that because they haven't got jobs, they'll never have jobs," Shannon explained. "Then the Gospel comes in and says something different: 'This whole world God is creating—it's for you, too. God has plans and purposes for you; God has created you with gifts and skills.' What hopes and dreams and aspirations do *they* have? What I want to do is see those realized" (Shannon, Personal interview 2).

Trees Connected at the Roots

Worship style and common history aren't all that binds St. Barnabas and Church@Five. Had this been a typical church plant, Kendal says, the question would have been, "When can we cut the umbilical cord? When can we shove this fledgling out of the nest and let it fly?" But St. Barnabas is maintaining its relationship with Church@Five financially as well as spiritually. Although giving is a core value, Church@Five will never pay for itself—and that poses no problem for the St. Barnabas leadership. "We recognize this is mission," Kendal said. "This is us giving out, and we're happy for that to happen" (Kendal, Personal interview 1).

Also linking the congregations is the governance structure. St. Barnabas's board, the Parochial Church Council, has set aside one seat for a Church@Five member. "We need to remember them, so we give them a kind of privileged position on PCC," said Markey. "The Church@Five voices remind us to look outside, beyond what happens in the main church building. They represent the poor more than St. Barnabas does, so they're a provocation to be more risky, to be more edgy, to be a bit less comfortable" (Markey).

Connected at a deep level, St. Barnabas and Church@Five inhabit a dual reality, unified and distinct. Church@Five is officially "a community congregation of St. Barnabas Church" ("Come As You Are To Church@Five"), as well as "a worshipping expression of the culture and the community that it's in," Shannon said (Shannon, Personal interview 1). She describes the relationship in terms of family. "I'm part of my extended family. We get together at Christmas and Easter; we look after one another and share vision for one another's lives," she said. "And then I've got my nuclear family. Well, that's St. B's and Church@Five" (Shannon, Personal interview 2). Kendal agrees with the family metaphor, though the perspective from St. Barnabas may be slightly different. "For a lot of St. Barnabas people, those are quite distant cousins at Church@Five," Kendal said. "They may have never met them, but they know they're over there" (Kendal, Personal interview 2).

Going and Growing

Another strain of boundary-breaking DNA that St. Barnabas and Church@Five share is an expectation of growth. Even Church@ Five, only five years old, is raising up missionaries from among the Strawberry Vale residents to take its model to another nearby housing estate. "It's part of our DNA that we replicate," Shannon said (Shannon, Personal interview 2). Markey sees the same call for St. Barnabas, whether it plays out in sponsoring foreign missionaries or meeting needs next door: "Living a life of mission doesn't mean moving to darkest Amazonia," he said. Markey notes the work of St. Barnabas's various missional communities—preparing food for homeless guests, visiting people in prison, or speaking to local members of Parliament about social justice issues. He says the missional relationship between the inherited church and the new expression is symbiotic: Church@Five "has been both a catalyst and a manifestation of something which lots of us have caught and said, 'This applies to us as well; we can do this'" (Markey).

For St. Barnabas, being sent into the world also means picking up and moving to a new, larger location. The congregation is several years into a capital campaign, "Go+Grow," to purchase the largest commercial building in its North Finchley area and renovate it as a new home for St. Barnabas—a home actually outside its historic parish boundaries. Worship and program have outgrown the 1914 structure, and its neighborhood location makes parking a challenge.

So the new building will include a parking structure and seating for five hundred, more than double the old church's capacity. The new worship space, called "the auditorium," is designed with a stage and rows of chairs arcing around it—and that's a theological statement. "The whole design of the old building is about the remoteness and grandeur of God," Kendal said, "whereas one of our hallmarks is that God can be known, and we can have intimacy with him. So the new space will feel very, very different" (Kendal, Personal interview 2). St. Barnabas expects construction and relocation to be completed in 2017.

Formed to Be a Blessing

Back on Strawberry Vale, Shannon sees great impact on a small scale, too—the housing estate being blessed one person at a time. She says Church@Five's mission statement—"bless, belong, believe, become"—describes a process of transforming individuals to transform their community. Church members came to Strawberry Vale simply to bless the estate first, "drawing inwards the people on the very outside," people wanting to be part of that blessing "almost not knowing what it's about," Shannon said. "As they're part of our community, they meet Jesus and they believe in him—and *then* the transformation happens and they become all that God has called them to be and do the things that God has called them to do," blessing Strawberry Vale and beyond (Shannon, Personal interview 1).

For Shannon, there's no time to lose with this kind of work. "There are hundreds and hundreds of these housing estates in London; and if we're going to make an inroad, we've got to be quick on it," she said. Church@Five "is a way of doing something authentic to reach out to these guys. By and large, they're not going to come into the churches. We've got to go" (Shannon, Personal interview 2).

ST. JAMES & EMMANUEL AND ABIDE, MANCHESTER, ENGLAND

Didsbury, a suburb south of Manchester, England, reminds me of my own church's neighborhood, Brookside in Kansas City. That may be due in part to the charming geographic miss on the sign of a KFC-inspired fast-food joint in Didsbury, "Kansas Fried Chicken." More than that, it's about charm paired with affluence. Pubs, coffeehouses, and specialty shops line Didsbury's main streets. The neighborhood features lovely homes of attorneys, physicians, media executives, and University of Manchester professors. Families juggle their kids' commitments to sports, music lessons, and horse riding. And it's not necessarily a place where people share their vulnerabilities or their hearts easily. "This is probably the richest area I've lived in as a Christian," says José Hacking, a member of St. James & Emmanuel, the Church of England's parish in Didsbury. "But this is the hardest area spiritually. When people are poor, they don't pretend because they have nothing. Here, there's a huge veneer" (Hacking).

So at St. James & Emmanuel, the boundaries to be challenged involve welcoming people in, building community, and cultivating a sense of belonging. Compounding those challenges is the fact that the church is actually two congregations—St. James, the original parish church dating from 1236; and Emmanuel, the "new" congregation carved out in 1858. Within these two congregations are four distinct worshiping communities: a 1662 Book of Common Prayer Eucharist at St. James; an "informal but traditional" family service at St. James; a somewhat raucous family service at Emmanuel with contemporary music, a praise band, and scores of excited kids; and a Sunday evening service at Emmanuel whose worship style changes every week of the month ("Services"). So the challenge is finding unity in all that diversity, said the Rev. Nick Bundock, rector. "We're very Anglican in that sense" (Bundock).

The Mustard Tree

Although that diversity could threaten to take St. James & Emmanuel in a hundred different directions, the congregation uses its different expressions to build a sense of belonging. Bundock sees its four worshiping communities and other community-facing ministries as branches of the mustard tree of God's kingdom, as described in Mark's Gospel: It "puts forth large branches so that the birds of the air can make nests in its shade" (4:32).

Those branches take several forms, some of which look more like "church" than others. Didsbury Church of England Primary School began in the back of St. James church more than four hundred years ago, and today the school's families make up a high proportion of the worshipers at Emmanuel. The school, and its partnership with the church, has been so successful that the congregation has started a second primary school about a mile northwest of Emmanuel to reach families the first school wasn't reaching.

Other branches of this mustard tree are church facilities. Emmanuel's Parish Centre houses church offices, a large gathering space, and other flexible spaces used for classes and group meetings. The large gathering space shelters foreign asylum seekers one day and night per week. The congregation also rents space for community use, including parties, receptions, meetings, classes, and dance lessons. The Parish Centre is relatively new, built in 2007; and fundraising for construction was a challenge. But according to churchwarden Vicki Long, it now pays for itself through rentals (Long). Emmanuel's former rectory also serves as a community resource, offering meeting space and housing the offices of eight local nonprofits.

The mustard tree's newest branch is a Youth Café in Emmanuel's entryway. It's a "social enterprise run by the church" as a separate charitable entity, Bundock says. That entity runs the café, and local groups gather there for coffee and community building. The groups register with the café, and any profits from their purchases go back to support those partner groups. "So we've created a space around coffee and hospitality that's friendly to community groups—a community-focused, not-for-profit business," Bundock says. The physical location in Emmanuel's building makes the church door not a barrier but a boundary crossing. "The café is in that liminal space—not in the church proper but in the foyer," a subtle and welcoming expression of the church's life (Bundock).

The point is to create space where people can feel they belong. "All we're called to do is to extend branches," Bundock explained. "If the birds of the air land on them, we're happy. And if they fly off again, we're happy. And if people become interested, and merge or blend into one of our Sunday things, we rejoice in that" (Bundock).

Renewing the Institution

Emmanuel has sometimes struggled to create community that puts leaves on its branches to shade the birds who land. The Sunday evening service especially suffered a few years ago. Parishioners say it had become cliquish and insular—and progressively smaller, eventually just a handful of people. So in 2011, St. James & Emmanuel called the Rev. Ben Edson, who had developed a fresh expression of church, Sanctus 1, in downtown Manchester. Emmanuel's Sunday evening congregation "was struggling for a sense of identity and yet alongside this there was a desire for authentic community and a deeper life of commitment to God and to one another," Edson writes (Edson, "Abide").

Working within an inherited expression of church was different from developing a freestanding fresh expression, but Edson saw a similar need—creating community that becomes church rather than waiting for worship to draw people in. "At St. James & Emmanuel, we still have the privilege of being an attractional church with weddings, baptisms, and the school," Edson said. "The two morning congregations can sit there, and people come. The evening congregation is the first here to engage with the post-Christian context" (Edson, Personal interview).

The primary place for that engagement is a community within the Sunday evening service—Abide, "the missional community of St. James & Emmanuel." When Edson arrived, he and about fifteen people from the Sunday evening service explored where it stood and what it needed. "We recognized that we wanted to be committed to one another in a common lifestyle, in mission and in prayer," Edson writes. "It's a community, it's missional, it has new monastic elements to it; but I think . . . it is ordinary people with ordinary lives, exploring and learning how to walk an extraordinary path together" (Edson, "Abide").

At the same time, Abide is very intentional about being part of St. James & Emmanuel. Edson couches the community's life in terms of "sodal" and "modal" models of church as described by George Lings, director of research for The Church Army in the UK. "Modal" refers to "the customary ways things are done," the inherited model of church most of us know. "Sodal" refers to "small and mobile" expressions of church like monastic communities and parachurch organizations—groups with "a significant sense of belonging, . . . high commitment and particular purpose" (Lings 1,2).

So Abide, as a community within the evening congregation, is "an expression of sodal within the modal," Edson said. It's intended to leaven the loaf of St. James & Emmanuel, not create something separate from it. "The mission of Abide is to strengthen the existing church family, working within the institution toward being a renewal of the institution" (Edson, Personal interview).

Rhythms of Grace

Part of that renewal comes in commitment to a rule of life known as the "five rhythms of grace," adopted from the Community of St. Chad in Lichfield, England. Similar to the five promises Episcopalians know from the Baptismal Covenant, the five rhythms "encourage us to live as believers in the real world, not in some kind of holy huddle," Edson writes (Edson, "Abide"). Each beginning with, "By God's grace," the five promises are: "Seek to be transformed into the likeness of Christ; be open to the presence, guidance and power of the Holy Spirit; set aside time for prayer, worship and spiritual reading; endeavour to be a gracious presence in the world, serving others and working for justice in human relationships and social structures; and sensitively share my faith with others, participating in God's mission both locally and globally" ("The Five Rhythms of Grace").

Abide members say they memorize the five rhythms or carry cards bearing them as a prayer aid; they're also encouraged to stop what they're doing and pray at noon each day. Abide corporate worship focuses on the five rhythms regularly. Crystallizing their ethos into a rule has an effect members see in their daily lives. "It makes you more aware of the people in the city who are not aware of church," Long said. "It does make you think how you react with people, how we can reach out to the community a bit more" (Long).

Community with Permeable Boundaries

Abide gathers twice a month, once for worship and once for a common meal. Among the eclectic services on Sunday evenings, the Abide service is the most contemplative. "We offer space to stop and reflect," Edson said. Although the worship is always Eucharistic, Edson draws on a variety of resources beyond authorized liturgies; worship from the Iona Community is a favorite source. "I start basically with a blank piece of paper," Edson said. "If there's something the community wants to explore, we'll construct a service around that theme" (Edson, Personal interview).

Preaching becomes an opportunity to build community as well as break open Scripture. Near the beginning of the service, Edson will often interview a worshiper about his or her journey, "teasing out things he's going to pick up and then invite the rest of the community to wrestle with," said Jason Powell, an ordination candidate on placement at St. James & Emmanuel. Later in the service, Edson will offer a "gentle challenge" about discipleship, Powell said, which often includes an invitation to some physical response, such as lighting candles, arranging small stones, or writing struggles on pieces of paper and burning them. The final part of the proclamation is Edson offering "the heavier chunk, where you're invited to really wrestle with something," Powell said (Powell).

The monthly meal is just as formative as worship. It's a potluck, so everyone feeds everyone else. But the feeding doesn't end with the meal; Abide members also share testimonials about their spiritual practice. "If we get to know one another and share those experiences, it builds us," Powell said. "Then we talk about different interpretations of those experiences and how we might understand God in them." Like the monthly worship, Abide's fellowship is open to anyone who wants to come. "The idea is to sit with someone you don't normally talk to, to break down those groups that form in churches," Powell explained. "We're trying to be much more of a holistic community" (Powell).

So Abide is an intentional community with very permeable boundaries. About sixty people come to a typical Abide service, and they range in age from their twenties to their seventies. Annually, people have the opportunity to commit themselves publicly to the community's rule of life, but "there's no membership list," said member Ben Jones. He described Abide simply as "a network of people committed to each other, practicing our faith a bit more intentionally" than other St. James & Emmanuel members might (B. Jones).

Mission Where You Are

Being "the missional community of St. James & Emmanuel" is still a work in progress. Abide is clearly missional in the sense of building the existing congregation. "A number of people have come in through Abide—it's been their doorway into the church," Edson said (Edson, Personal interview). As a group, the Abide community also takes a turn each month staffing the congregation's ministry sheltering foreign asylum seekers, and it provides volunteer support for the Youth Café. But Abide's greatest missional effect so far is in the hearts of the people it forms. The rule of life and the deep sense of community equip individuals to be everyday missionaries, being "a gracious presence in the world" and "sensitively shar[ing] faith with others" ("The Five Rhythms of Grace"). As Edson said, reflecting the mustard-tree image, "We want to deepen our roots in prayer and extend our arms more to people outside the church" (Edson, Personal interview).

How that looks, on the ground, varies from person to person and moment to moment. Hacking, who hasn't always felt at home at St. James & Emmanuel or in Didsbury, said she's felt called to befriend young pregnant women in her neighborhood and even to bring "notice sheets" (church announcements) to people nearby, inviting them to be part of the church community. "To me, the monastic thing isn't about looking out my window at my beautiful view of the sky and the trees," Hacking said. "It's about listening to God and asking, 'What are your priorities for me today?' Quite often, I end up bumping into people and having a coffee and hearing them share something on their heart. My missional community is a place where God calls individuals to do what he wants them to do, where he's placed them" (Hacking).

ST. PAUL'S AND CENTER, RICHMOND, VIRGINIA

Walking down Grace Street to St. Paul's Episcopal Church in Richmond, Virginia, you can see why it's been known for decades as the "cathedral of the Confederacy." Its stunning 1845 Greek revival building sits literally across the street from the Virginia State Capitol, the meeting place of the Confederate Congress. Gen. Robert E. Lee worshiped there, and Confederate President Jefferson Davis was a confirmed member ("History"). St. Paul's altar missal from the early 1860s, displayed at the American Civil War Museum in Richmond, marks the historical moment in longhand: In the collect "for the President . . . and all in Civil Authority," the words "United States" are scratched out, with "Confederate States" written carefully in the margin.

But well before the Charleston, South Carolina, church shootings in the summer of 2015 and St. Paul's painstaking work to remove images of the Stars and Bars from its historical markers (Vestry, St. Paul's Episcopal Church, Richmond, VA), St. Paul's was already a reconciling force, living into the hope of its Grace Street address. Along with the remaining Confederate iconography inside the church, you notice a portrait on the wall that, at first glance, seems like it must be a mistake: the Rev. John Shelby Spong, St. Paul's rector from 1969 until 1976, when he was elected bishop of Newark. The story is told of Spong taking down the Confederate battle flag from St. Paul's portico on one of his first Sundays as rector. "He just walked out and took it down," said the Rev. Melanie Mullen, downtown missioner at St. Paul's. "The church wrote a letter to the paper saying, 'We think it's OK to integrate'" (Mullen, Personal interview 2). Today, that progressive witness continues. St. Paul's sponsors Richmond's Pridefest and Transgender Day of Remembrance, even as it's home to many civic leaders whose family roots and fortunes go back to slavery days. "The congregation is almost paradoxical," said Sam Jackson, a thirty-something parishioner. "It's full of people who are very conservative in some ways but also very liberal—socialists in seersucker. You see more bow ties than you can shake a stick at" (Jackson).

Downtown Mission, Then and Now

Early in its history, St. Paul's discerned a call to break down boundaries between the church and people living and working in its downtown neighborhood. It began Lenten weekday worship in a downtown store in 1887 and has long participated in feeding ministries with other downtown churches ("History"). By the 1950s and 1960s, as Richmond's population moved toward the suburbs, several downtown churches followed. But St. Paul's received a gift of the western half of its city block and decided to double down on downtown, building a parish house and parking structure and offering new connecting points, like the Eyes on Richmond fall speaker series ("2015 Eyes on Richmond") and jazz lunches in the spring.

In the past decade, Richmond has seen a downtown residential renaissance among younger adults, augmenting the tens of thousands who drive in daily for work. "The harvest is plentiful," said St. Paul's rector, the Rev. Wallace Adams-Riley. "How could we not respond to that for the sake of, and in the name of, the Gospel?" So in 2012, St. Paul's called Mullen, then a new priest, as its downtown missioner. "We said from the start this was going to be experimental," Adams-Riley said. "The core thing is, how do we open new doors and enter into relationship with folks we otherwise may well not get to know?" (Adams-Riley).

Mullen said her job description began as "five pages of poetry, trying to include everybody in the community" (Mullen, Personal interview 1). During seminary, Mullen had taken courses in church-based community organizing, so meeting people and building connections was a sweet spot. "But I didn't have anything to plug people into, once I went out and met them," she said. "There are lots of people here in downtown, but what are we connecting them to? What are we offering them?" (Mullen, Personal interview 2).

Organizing a Worshiping Community

Adams-Riley wanted St. Paul's to create a new worship opportunity as a connecting point for young adults in downtown. At the same time, lay leaders such as vestry member Brian Levey were exploring alternative worship with Mullen. Though Mullen wasn't called specifically to start a new service, the planning group saw it as a way to provide "some kind of content," Levey said. "We had to have a starting point" (Levey).

Mullen, Levey, and their team began by testing worship possibilities, including prayer services in city parks and Stations of the Cross at the downtown farmers' market. But logistical considerations brought them back to St. Paul's. Mullen had seen many approaches to alternative worship, including presentations from the Rev. Stephanie Spellers at the Crossing in Boston. Levey, a former Baptist minister, was looking to provide interpersonal connection; others on the team wanted a contemplative experience; others wanted an arts focus. The initial offering, in Lent 2012, was simply open-space prayer stations in the church after work. Later test services combined Scripture reading; instrumental music and chant; participatory prayer such as lighting candles, walking a labyrinth, writing prayers on dissolving paper, viewing projected images, and meditating with icons; and dinner afterward, including feedback from the worshipers (Mullen, Personal interview 2).

Mullen also gathered people she had met from the neighborhood—"people with tattoos and piercings, homeless people, business folks, and apartment dwellers"—for listening sessions. These were "fishbowl exercises," with downtown neighbors responding to questions as church members listened in. "We were finding out who's there and how comfortable they are with the church," Mullen said—"what are you afraid of about church, what's meaningful or not, what makes it relevant or not, what do you wish the church would be and do?" (Mullen, Personal interview 1).

Finding St. Paul's Center

The experiments and feedback have led to Center, weekly contemplative worship and table fellowship that began in the summer of 2014. The gathering happens on Wednesdays, after work, in an atrium with a glass ceiling between the church and the parish house. Mullen sets up four or five prayer stations, as well as a circle of chairs in one corner. Worshipers hear Scripture (a selection from the weekly lectionary) and a complementary reading from another faith tradition or secular poetry. Then Mullen poses a question or two and rings a bell to begin about thirty minutes of open-space time accompanied by an instrumentalist, usually violin, cello, or accordion. Worshipers can remain in the circle or visit the prayer stations as they choose. "I have five or six go-to stations that rotate, but I'm always finding new ones," Mullen said. "I look for things like braiding cloth or yarn, tubs of water with candles or dissolving paper, rocks, votive candles, praying the newspaper, writing notes to people, tastings. I'm always digging things up. My office is a mess, like somebody's school exploded" (Mullen, Personal interview 2).

Then Mullen leads a reflective conversation about the readings and contemplative time, followed by Prayers of the People led by a cantor. Worship officially closes with the Peace, but the experience then morphs into dinner as the group moves into the next room to share soup, bread, and wine. Center never actually celebrates Eucharist, but the experience is one of deep communion. "In Christianity, we talk a lot about breaking the bread," said Nick Courtney, a young Center regular. "But that little wafer isn't really much bread-breaking. Center is truly a bonding experience, sharing a good meal together and talking about what we experienced during worship" (Courtney). Mullen said this need for relationship kept coming up in interviews with neighborhood residents. "We'd hear, 'I'm lonely,' over and over and over again. They want ways to get together with people, so the dinner was really important" (Mullen, Personal interview 2). That kind of relationship building, and the theological reflection that springs from it, is the dinner's only agenda. "We talked about structuring the conversation and using questions to prompt discussion," Mullen said. The participants declined. "They were like, 'We'd rather talk about drag queens'" (Mullen, Personal interview 2).

"Left-Handed" Downtown Connection

Center is only one effort among several ways St. Paul's connects with its downtown neighbors, including block parties, music and poetry events, and book discussions in a coffeehouse. And Center is relatively small, about twenty people a week. But in a parish constantly busy with one program after another, Center breaks down boundaries in a new, more contemplative way. "The intention was to create space for people who live and work downtown, a place they can stop in and engage with God and community," said Beth Burton, a Center participant. "In a sense, it's the same model the church uses serving lunch for homeless people—just a different audience with different needs. They come here, and they sit, and they just be—and that's what they want. I can come here and be a real person, a whole person, not just the person who wears nice dresses at Christmas and Easter" (Burton).

For Burton, Center is like an art studio in the sense that it invites people to experience being co-creators with God. "We have this job, if you will, of trying to figure out how these ideas in Scripture and poetry and art relate to each other," Burton said. "I love how Melanie gets the senses involved in making something— 'engage in this activity, and see what happens'" (Burton).

In practicing contemplation, creativity, and relationship with other spiritual pilgrims, Courtney and Jackson say they find their deepest connection with God. They worship at St. Paul's 11:15 a.m. Sunday service, too—the parish's highest liturgy, with full choir and traditional hymns. But Center is "the holy of holies," Courtney said—"the more serious prayer, the more serious spiritual connection" (Courtney). Said Jackson: "We're individuals at Center, rather than members of a corporate body" (Jackson).

Through Center, St. Paul's is building muscle, finding a new—and very old—way to connect with its neighbors. "Like any church, St. Paul's has its strengths," Mullen said. It's "right-handed" in its activist, energetic, programmatic approach to being church. "But it hasn't used its left much," Mullen said—until now (Mullen, Personal interview 2).

Building Community or Growing the Church?

But will Center, or the other elements of St. Paul's downtown mission, grow the church? And is that the litmus test of success? Levey, who served on the vestry when Mullen was called, remembers the congregation understood the move was risky. "We've designated money for a certain amount of time geared toward downtown mission without an expectation of return on investment," he said. "I would say we took a pretty big leap of faith in that." Levey acknowledges that opinions differ about whether Center, and downtown mission generally, should be expected to increase membership and pledging, traditional marks of congregational success. "With downtown mission being a fresh expression of community and faith, I don't know why we would expect that to turn into traditional membership and participation," Levey said. "But isn't building spiritual community still growing the church? If those people don't serve on committees, does that mean they aren't participating members of the faith community? There are a lot of people who go to the main services who don't serve on committees or pledge" (Levey).

Adams-Riley acknowledges that downtown mission hasn't led directly to new pledging units. But, he said, "People have joined us since we entered into downtown mission, and I think downtown mission is a part of why they came to be part of our community." Adams-Riley sees an artificial tension between ministries that seem geared to build up a religious institution—precisely what many unchurched and de-churched people disrespect—and ministries that altruistically serve people in the community. "There's a worry that we're going to seem imperialistic or self-serving—that we really want you to join our church so we can keep our numbers up and keep our giving strong," he said. "If it's really of Christ, mission, by its nature, is not self-serving. But then, after wrestling with all that, I bounce back and say, 'Wait a minute. I believe in St. Paul's. I believe God is doing something good through this church in downtown Richmond. Of course we want it to grow'" (Adams-Riley).

Even in a congregation that isn't struggling with survival, leaders see the financial challenges to inherited models of church. Adams-Riley noted that replacing a "classic" pledge from a long-time Episcopalian typically takes three to five pledges from new members, who often don't carry the cultural DNA of pledging. And the coming "death tsunami" among the Baby Boomers will intensify the financial pressure all the more (Adams-Riley). As Mullen said, "I know my job isn't about 'butts in the seats,' but after just a few months at St. Paul's, I was getting questions about when we would see more butts in the seats" (Mullen, Personal interview 1).

Yet, while congregations wrestle with these realities, efforts like St. Paul's downtown mission slowly and quietly gather people into blessed community—people who likely wouldn't have come together otherwise. "We have a very eclectic group in Center," Jackson explained (Jackson). Courtney fleshed it out: "We have women in their late sixties who've been traditional Episcopalians all their lives, and we have young gay men who do burlesque shows. And we've become a rather tight-knit little group" (Courtney).

THREE CONGREGATIONS, TWO NEW EXPRESSIONS, AND SHARED GOVERNANCE, ST. MARY'S COUNTY, MARYLAND

As you drive down Highway 249 in rural St. Mary's County, Maryland, you see a small, familiar metal sign in the Valley Lee

Post Office yard—"The Episcopal Church Welcomes You," with an arrow pointing down a secondary road. A couple of miles along that road is a similar sign for St. George's Episcopal Church, a building on the National Register of Historic Places and a congregation that in 2015 convened its 378th annual meeting. St. George's has two driveways, one leading to the old church and graveyard, and the other leading to the parish hall—but at first glance, a visitor wouldn't know which one to take. As might be said about St. George's, so it's true about The Episcopal Church in St. Mary's County generally: If you're "supposed" to be here, you *know* the way in.

Maryland's founders landed in St. Mary's County in 1634, some of them bringing the Church of England with them. So, both in congregational and civic leadership, "this is a place with old names," explained the Rev. Greg Syler, rector of St. George's. But beginning with the opening of the Patuxent River Naval Air Station in 1943, change and economic development have come to what had been "a tiny country county," Syler said. Today, among the 110,000 people in St. Mary's County are seven Episcopal congregations, most with deep history and all with small numbers. "This county is shifting between the old and the new, and The Episcopal Church in St. Mary's County is *old*. Just look at our front yard," Syler said, pointing to headstones from centuries back. "So even if people *wanted* to be Episcopalians, they'd have a hard time if they came here and they weren't a Mattingly or a Jarboe or a Morris" (Syler, Personal interview 2).

Since 2013, leaders in three St. Mary's County congregations have been trying to move past both external and internal boundaries to open up The Episcopal Church in new ways. They saw barriers in worship and governance keeping their churches looking inward rather than moving out in mission to their growing county.

Gather Eat Pray

For some young adults, these congregations and their inherited worship style—the same liturgy every week, music from the *Hymnal 1982*, and traditional, one-way preaching—had come to feel stale. They were also looking for worship that engaged their children, rather than sending them off to Sunday school. "We wanted worship that was nontraditional but still had elements of the Episcopal tradition, worship that would be attractive to young adults and families," said Eva Thompson, a young adult and a former member of Ascension Episcopal Church in Lexington Park, Maryland (Thompson). Another young adult leader and senior warden of Ascension, Tom McCarthy, put a finer point on it, remembering conversations with younger visitors in the past few years: "They say, 'Is it always an hour and a quarter? Do you always use all the verses and sing so many songs? Could we do some new music? Do you always read all the names off the prayer list?' They all asked at least three of those questions, and they didn't get the answers they wanted. So they haven't been back" (McCarthy).

Thompson and McCarthy also felt the physical settings—quaint old churches with box pews—could be off-putting. "Church is threatening to some who had a bad experience growing up," Thompson said. "If you say, 'Come to church,' you've already lost some people. If they want to find God in a neutral location, then by God, we should be able to provide that for them" (Thompson).

So in 2013, the young adult leaders met with clergy from St. George's, Ascension, and Trinity in St. Mary's City and created a new monthly worship opportunity—Gather Eat Pray, inspired by the dinner-church model of St. Lydia's in Brooklyn, New York (stlydias.org). Beginning in November 2013, the service basically inverted the shape of the Eucharist. The gathering began with an improvised Eucharistic prayer and Communion among worshipers seated around a table. Then came dinner and a Scripture reading, after which children would have their own activity while clergy led a discussion. Then the kids returned for prayers, songs, and a dismissal. "It felt like a dinner party with church," Syler said (Syler, Personal interview 1). Unfortunately, the location (a conference center) felt "sterile," Thompson said, and the sound of the kids in the same room overwhelmed the adults' conversation (Thompson).

Those factors, plus expensive rent, led Gather Eat Pray to move into members' homes, with both positive and negative results. The price was right, and the gathering felt authentic and intimate—"reminiscent of what the apostles were doing in the early church," Thompson said. At its "most magical," she said, the discussion *was* the proclamation of the Word—"improvisational, like jazz" (Thompson). But clergy from the three parishes led the discussion with different styles, and sometimes "the guided discussion was a lot of guidance and little discussion," McCarthy remembered (McCarthy). The intimate setting also had its drawbacks: "We lost some people there, because they just felt weird going to someone else's home, especially for the first time," Thompson said (Thompson).

Finally, Gather Eat Pray moved to a small art studio in a converted house. It offered a neutral but intimate location, and the art supplies inspired great activities with elementary-aged kids. But tending the toddlers in the same space—or arranging supervision in another room—revealed an inherent problem: meeting the needs of kids of all ages, and adults, in a shared worship setting. "Those of us with toddlers were more antiliturgical," McCarthy said. "It's hard to pray when you have a screaming or fidgety kid on your lap." He also noted that what draws in one family may cause another to stay away: "Seven-year-olds shouldn't be playing with candles and paints near toddlers" (McCarthy).

Who's It For?

Beneath the struggles of worship design ran a deeper conflict: Who's the effort for? Gather Eat Pray stopped meeting after one year primarily because the people involved couldn't agree whether it was a small group or a new worshiping community. For the Rev. Erin Betz-Shank, who served as St. Mary's County missioner for the Diocese of Washington, DC, and oversaw Gather Eat Pray, the identity question sprang from the ministry's purpose. "You have to start with the right intent, which is to build the kingdom," she said. "The way this group started was, 'I don't like my Rite II worship on Sunday.' If we had started this group saying, 'Let's talk about ways we can reach new people who might not walk into our parishes on Sunday,' that would have changed the conversation." Eventually, Betz-Shank said, Gather Eat Pray ran aground on the rocks of its founders' preferences. "Sometimes people can be so focused on 'this is what I want' that it pulls you in so many directions beside forward" (Betz-Shank).

As Gather Eat Pray was winding down, in the fall of 2014, St. George's and Ascension began a new collaboration, along with a local United Methodist congregation, to take them outside the church walls: Thirsty Theology, a monthly gathering for drinks and theological reflection at a local bar. There's no worship, but each gathering begins with a presentation on a spiritual topic to get the conversation going. Most of the participants are at least nominal members of one of the congregations, but the gathering is helping to break down a long-bemoaned Episcopalian boundary: "It's been the one place where members will—and, in fact, do—invite and bring their friends, people who have little to no connection with a faith community," Syler said. "They won't bring their friends to church, or maybe even think to offer it; but they will bring them to a pub on Tuesday night" (Syler, Email correspondence 2).

Whether as a worshiping community, a pub conversation, or something else, the intent is to give The Episcopal Church in southern Maryland a different face than box pews and tombstones. Thompson and McCarthy describe ministries like Gather Eat Pray and Thirsty Theology as parallel developments—missional efforts in cooperation with existing parish life. It's like Western and complementary medicine, Thompson says: "Separately, each can enhance people's relationship with Christ, but imagine what they can do together" (Thompson).

But parallel developments don't necessarily fit neatly into inherited structures or practices. Which parish's records should get the attendance figures? And are these ministries intended as gateways to build specific congregations? Syler says the clergy's intent has been to reach unchurched people through a collaborative Episcopal presence, rather than building particular parishes (Syler, Personal interview 1). Les Taylor, former junior warden at Ascension, agrees: "If we aren't reaching unchurched people in our pews, how do we? So the point of Gather Eat Pray was, 'Can we go to where they are? Can we do things they like?' Not necessarily to bring more people into our church, but to church some more people" (L. Taylor).

Collaborative Governance?

Maybe the only thing more potentially conflicted than shared ministry is shared governance, but these parishes have taken that journey, too. During development of Gather Eat Pray, leaders began outlining a structure for sharing some ministries and financial operations, creating a level of authority between the parish and the bishop's office—a Multi-Parish Council of clergy and vestry leaders from each parish. They sought to create a collaborative culture among the congregations so they could plan to share major expenses, such as clergy, support staff, and facilities costs. "The idea was, let's have a conversation," said Tom DeSelms, former senior warden at Ascension. "Let's share the contract for a copier. Let's share the gardening. When the secretary leaves or retires, maybe we don't need another one full-time; maybe it could be ten hours a week here and ten hours a week there" (DeSelms).

The most emotionally charged proposal was that the Multi-Parish Council would recommend how to move forward when a rector left a member church. The Rev. Sherrill Page, former rector of Ascension, described it as a way to build collaboration and trust among the parishes before crises hit, "so that, when the time comes, there can be a deeper conversation about how the future could look, not limited to a one-clergy-one-parish model" (Page). Not surprisingly, the risk of diminished autonomy caused a lot of fear. "You're taking away some of the power of each vestry. It's full of potholes and power and control," DeSelms said (DeSelms). Ultimately, Trinity parish pulled out of the agreement, leaving St. George's and Ascension to move ahead together. They formed the Multi-Parish Council in early 2015—and the timing was auspicious. As it happened, Page had spoken more than she knew in advocating for collaboration *before* the crisis of a rector's departure. In early 2015, she died in office. In the resulting fear and anxiety, the Multi-Parish Council was reimagined as a

Discernment Council to "facilitate the possibility of what's next" for the two parishes, Syler said (Syler, E-mail correspondence 1). In late 2015, the council recommended that Ascension and St. George's yoke rather than Ascension calling a new rector to replace Page, and both vestries agreed. The shape of their collaboration will be hammered out into a formal covenant, but it will likely include a shared vestry or additional layer of leadership, separate finances, shared clergy, and worship at both churches. In a letter to St. George's, Syler explained that a yoking relationship would let the parishes put resources toward becoming "more outward-focused, . . . a necessary first step" toward "the model of church we feel God calling us to be" (Syler, "(Re)Making History: God's Future for Our Church"). That kind of a church "gets out of our four walls a whole lot more," Syler said. "That is the point [of sharing leadership]. Otherwise, it's about a dying church trying to shore up what resources it has" (Syler, Personal interview 2).

Leaven in the Loaf

In a place where families have been doing church in much the same way since settlers stepped off the ships in 1634 (literally just down the hill from Trinity Church in St. Mary's City), Gather Eat Pray, Thirsty Theology, and the Multi-Parish Council have been giant steps forward in leavening the missional loaf and creating a nimbler church. For these parishes, sharing ministry, governance, and clergy is frightening. But these have been necessary steps toward remembering, in an anamnetic way, the Church's primary mission. As Syler says, "Communities of faith such as St. George's have had to face down the demons in our common lives, asking the question, 'Fundamentally, for whom does the Church exist?' If the Church's primary mission is still being chaplain to the established membership, then the missional question is something of a threat. But if the Church's primary mission is to gain new believers, nurture the faithful, and build up the kingdom of God, that changes the focus." Sharing ministries and governance, he concludes, "has the capacity, like grist in the mill, to make us confront this question" (Syler, Email correspondence 2).

In a traditional context—as in The Episcopal Church generally—inertia is probably the greatest enemy, perhaps second only to apathy. But in St. Mary's County, the ball is now rolling. Gather Eat Pray and Thirsty Theology have been "great opportunities to do something in the name of doing something," Syler explained. "Along with the rest of the world, St. Mary's County is radically shifting. The established names still kind of run the place, but now their children and grandchildren aren't picking up the mantle. This is a county where the old is on the way out and the new is on the rise" (Syler, Personal interview 2). And "the new" weren't born knowing where to find the church driveway among the tombstones.

References

Adams-Riley, Wallace. Personal interview by John Spicer. November 5, 2014.

"Anglo-Catholic." Accessed October 5, 2015. *http://www.stpaulseattle. org/spirituality/anglo-catholic.*

Bell, Missy. Personal interview by John Spicer. September 21, 2014.

Betz-Shank, Erin. Personal interview by John Spicer. August 26, 2014.

Bloom, Lara. Personal interview by John Spicer. October 14, 2014.

Bundock, Nick. Personal interview by John Spicer. October 24, 2014.

Burton, Beth. Personal interview by John Spicer. November 5, 2014.

Celebrate! Planning Group. Interview by John Spicer. October 10, 2014.

"Come As You Are To Church@Five." Accessed November 2, 2015. *http://www.stbarnabas.co.uk/Groups/162776/St_Barnabas_Church/ Community/Church_Five/Church_Five.aspx.*

"Council." Accessed August 15, 2015. *http://www.thecrossingboston. org/getinvolved/council.*

Courtney, Nick. Personal interview by John Spicer. November 2, 2014.

Crossing Leadership Structure Task Force. *Leadership Structure Task Force Report.* Boston: The Crossing, 2013.

Davidson, Helen. Personal interview by John Spicer. October 19, 2014.

DeSelms, Tom. Personal interview by John Spicer. November 7, 2014.

Devitt, Suni. Personal interview by John Spicer. September 21, 2014.

Eaton, Kate. Personal interview 1 by John Spicer. June 2, 2014.

———. Personal interview 2 by John Spicer. September 20, 2014.

———. "Services." Accessed August 31, 2015. *http://www.mishkhah. com/about/services/.*

Eaton, Peter. Personal interview by John Spicer. September 20, 2014.

Edson, Ben. "Abide." Last modified October 22, 2012. Accessed November 15, 2015. *https://www.freshexpressions.org.uk/stories/abide.*

———. Personal interview by John Spicer. May 1, 2014.

Everett, Isaac. Personal interview 1 by John Spicer. May 8, 2014.

———. Personal interview 2 by John Spicer. September 5, 2014.

"FAQ." Accessed September 12, 2015. *http://www.portlandabbey.org/ about/faq.*

"The Five Rhythms of Grace." Accessed November 12, 2015. *http://www. stjamesandemmanuel.org/the-five-rhythms-of-grace.*

Griffin, Laura. Personal interview by John Spicer. October 4, 2014.

Hacking, José. Personal interview by John Spicer. October 25, 2014.

Hartsuff, Jadon. Personal interview 1 by John Spicer. June 12, 2014.

———. Personal interview 2 by John Spicer. September 21, 2014.

"History." Accessed November 25, 2015. *http://www.stpaulsrva.org/ about/history.*

"History and Mission: The Cathedral Today." Accessed August 15, 2015. *http://www.stpaulboston.org/welcome/historyandmission.*

Jackson, Sam. Personal interview by John Spicer. November 2, 2014.

Jones, Ann Lindou. *Glory in the Wilderness: The Art of Saint John's Cathedral Denver, Colorado, 1911–2011.* Winter Park, CO: Guest-Guide Publications, 2011.

Jones, Ben. Personal interview by John Spicer. October 24, 2014.

Keith, Nathan. Personal interview by John Spicer. September 19, 2014.

Kendal, Henry. Personal interview 1 by John Spicer. July 8, 2014.

———. Personal interview 2 by John Spicer. October 16, 2014.

Kovar, Liz. Personal interview by John Spicer. October 19, 2014.

Kueter, Larry. Personal interview by John Spicer. October 7, 2014.

Kurdzeil, Annie. Personal interview by John Spicer. September 8, 2014.

Levey, Brian. Personal interview by John Spicer. November 3, 2014.

Lings, George. "Why Modality and Sodality Thinking Is Vital to Understand Future Church." *Church Army: Talks and Presentations.* Accessed November 16, 2015. *http://www.churcharmy.org.uk/Publisher/ File.aspx?ID=138339.*

"Liturgical Music." Accessed August 29, 2015. *http://www.sjcathedral.org/Music/LiturgicalMusic.*

Long, Vicki. Personal interview by John Spicer. October 26, 2014.

Low, Georgann. Personal interview by John Spicer. September 21, 2014.

Markey, Sam. Personal interview by John Spicer. October 19, 2014.

McCarthy, Tom. Personal interview by John Spicer. November 10, 2014.

"Missional Communities." Accessed October 31, 2015. *http://www.stbarnabas.co.uk/Groups/170546/St_Barnabas_Church/Whats_on/Missional_Communities/Missional_Communities.aspx#.VjUFNFWrTIU.*

Montoya, Shane. Personal interview by John Spicer. September 4, 2014.

Morgan, Justin. Personal interview by John Spicer. September 29, 2014.

Mullen, Melanie. Personal interview 1 by John Spicer. April 3, 2014.

———. Personal interview 2 by John Spicer. November 3, 2014.

Page, Sherrill. Personal interview by John Spicer. November 7, 2014.

"Parish History." Accessed October 5, 2015. *http://www.stpaulseattle.org/our-community/parish-history.*

Pommerenke, Martin. Personal interview by John Spicer. October 3, 2014.

Poulter, Josie. Personal interview by John Spicer. October 19, 2014.

Powell, Jason. Personal interview by John Spicer. October 25, 2014.

Ruffle, Wendy. Personal interview 1 by John Spicer. June 10, 2014.

———. Personal interview 2 by John Spicer. October 10, 2014.

"Services." Accessed December 15, 2015. *http://www.stjamesandemmanuel.org/services.*

Shand, Priscilla. Personal interview by John Spicer. September 19, 2014.

Shannon, Helen. Personal interview 1 by John Spicer. July 8, 2014.

———. Personal interview 2 by John Spicer. October 16, 2014.

Skelton, Melissa. Personal interview by John Spicer. September 10, 2014.

Spellers, Stephanie. Personal interview by John Spicer. September 10, 2014.

———. *Radical Welcome: Embracing God, The Other, and the Spirit of Transformation.* New York: Church Publishing, 2006.

St. John's Cathedral. "Welcome (brochure)." Denver: St. John's Cathedral, n.d.

"St. John's Cathedral Choir School." Accessed August 29, 2015. *http://www.sjcathedral.org/Music/ChildrenYouthChoirs.*

Steinke, Paul. Personal interview 1 by John Spicer. June 26, 2014.

————. Personal interview 2 by John Spicer. October 5, 2014.

Stevens, Karin. Personal interview by John Spicer. October 5, 2014.

Streit, John P. Personal interview 1 by John Spicer. July 24, 2014.

————. Personal interview 2 by John Spicer. September 5, 2014.

Sukraw, Tracy J. "Renovations and St. John's merger bring renewal to Cathedral Church of St. Paul." Last modified May 6, 2014. *Episcopal Diocese of Massachusetts: Answering God's Urgent Call. Together.* Accessed December 30, 2015. *http://www.diomass.org/diocesan-news/renovations-and-st-johns-merger-bring-renewal-cathedral-church-st-paul.*

Syler, Greg. E-mail correspondence 1 with John Spicer. December 15, 2015.

————. Email correspondence 2 with John Spicer. December 17, 2015.

————. Personal interview 1 by John Spicer. May 1, 2014.

————. Personal interview 2 by John Spicer. November 7, 2014.

————. "(Re)Making History: God's Future for Our Church." Last modified November 12, 2015. St. George's Episcopal Church, Valley Lee, MD. Accessed December 15, 2015. *http://www.stgeorges valleylee.org/sites/default/files/%28Re%29Making%20History%20 follow-through%2C%20a%20Message%20from%20Fr.%20 Greg%20-%20Thursday%2C%2012%20Nov.%202015.pdf.*

Taylor, Les. Personal interview by John Spicer. November 11, 2014.

Taylor, Mark. Personal interview by John Spicer. October 3, 2014.

Thompson, Eva. Personal interview by John Spicer. November 10, 2014.

"2015 Eyes on Richmond." Accessed November 25, 2015. *http://www. stpaulsrva.org/serve/outreach/eyes-on-richmond.*

Vestry, St. Paul's Episcopal Church, Richmond, VA. "Motion." Accessed November 30, 2015. *http://files.ctctcdn.com/1528f9709e/b7f406ee-6 bcb-4ddb-88aa-6e9aff2cb78b.pdf.*

Ward, Karen. E-mail correspondence with John Spicer. January 30, 2015.

————. Personal interview 1 by John Spicer. July 10, 2014.

————. Personal interview 2 by John Spicer. September 30, 2014.

Williams, Paul. Personal interview 1 by John Spicer. July 17, 2014.

3

Where's the Mission in Your DNA?

"We are ambassadors for Christ, since God is making his appeal through us; we entreat you on behalf of Christ, be reconciled to God." —2 Corinthians 5:20

THE NINE CONGREGATIONS I VISITED don't seem to have much in common. Even the two whose new expressions of church are most similar—Tewkesbury Abbey and St. Barnabas in London—barely seem to be worshiping in the same tradition on Sunday mornings. But these nine stories are much more similar than they might seem, regardless of the differences in size, location, or liturgical style. All of these congregations have stepped outside their boundaries and gone to the edges of their comfort zones, finding people to love they wouldn't have found otherwise.

Making a journey like that calls for a hundred decisions. But across these congregations' experiences, I heard people reflecting on five questions particularly:

- Where's the mission in our DNA?
- Whom are we trying to reach—and how?
- What expression of ministry is God trying to create?
- How will we empower strong leadership and plan for governance?
- How will we identify success and failure?

Getting the answers right—or at least asking them in good faith—makes the difference between having a nice idea and bringing blessing to God's world.

Mission in DNA or Mission as DNA?

In an earlier Episcopal day, we called the present expression of God's people "the Church militant." Though it may sound overly militaristic to our ears, the phrase captured the sense that God's people are to be active, even assertive, in incarnating God's rule and reign as revealed in the relational life, kenotic death, and victorious resurrection of Jesus Christ. As Jesus's followers, we're here to be deployed as ambassadors of God's reconciling work.

Rather than the "Church militant," we might today call it the "Church missional"—but that would be redundant. Church *is* mission. We are the *ecclesia*, the assembly, a Roman concept the early Christians turned on its head. *Ecclesia* originally implied an assembly of solid citizens, the elite who sat as the city councils of the Roman Empire. As the early Christians took the meaning of *kyrios* (Lord, in the sense of Caesar's divinity) and applied it to the risen Jesus instead, so our forebears took the meaning of *ecclesia* and turned it upside down: an assembly of all, including the poor, the powerless, and the slaves (Mobsby 81–82), as well as the dealers in "purple cloth" and other elites (Acts 16:14). And that *ecclesia* was empowered by the Holy Spirit not to build up institutions of governance but to go—to bear witness, in word and deed, to Christ's loving death, resurrection, and lordship. In other words, this assembly assembled to disassemble and engage people with whom God had placed them in relationship (Goodhew, Roberts, and Volland 7–13).

In today's *ecclesia*, when a new assembly is assembled, it begins at a missional advantage (which its founders can take or leave behind). A new congregation has the opportunity to establish its missional DNA from the very start, without the baggage of decades (or centuries) of genetic mutation. In my context, the Kansas City metro area, the preeminent example is the United Methodist Church of the Resurrection (COR). COR was founded by the Rev. Adam Hamilton in 1990 and famously began meeting in a funeral home in extreme south Kansas City. COR did excellent work to identify a permanent location and understand its cultural context. It was also blessed with an amazingly talented founding pastor. Among Hamilton's gifts is a laser-like focus on claiming and living into COR's purpose: "to build a Christian community where non-religious and nominally religious people are becoming deeply committed Christians" ("About Resurrection"). In creating that community, Hamilton and the COR lay leadership had no antimissional mutations to overcome; and the clarity of their call is one element of COR's astonishing growth. Today, it's a mainline megachurch, with four campuses in the Kansas City area and a total of 18,700 members (Montgomery).

Existing congregations come with existing DNA, the identities and proclivities formed across decades or centuries. Sometimes that wiring sends them, and their members, out in new ways, such as what's happening at Tewkesbury Abbey. Sometimes, not so much. Usually, of course, it's a mixed bag. In my congregation, St. Andrew's in Kansas City, Missouri, we're blessed with missional DNA from our founding—a new plant in 1913, on the edge of town, placed in the heart of what would become one of the city's premiere residential neighborhoods, beginning life in the back room of a grocery store. At the height of American Christendom, in the 1950s and 1960s, St. Andrew's helped lead the way; at one point it was the nation's third largest Episcopal congregation. Not surprisingly, that status along with a Christendom mindset allowed some institutional and entitlement DNA to form as well. But the most passionate memories of St. Andrew's, past its golden age, relate to the evangelism, service, and fiery preaching the congregation knew with the Rev. Jeffrey Black in the 1980s and 1990s. Today, mission and establishment vie for the center ring.

Of course, most of the congregations I visited face a similar dynamic. But among them, I found a common trait as they seek to become the churches God is calling them to be: Each has moved to break down its boundaries in ways that are true to missional strands deep in its DNA. Each is following a path whose outlines it already knows. It's part of living "an integrated life, not chasing after things," said the Rt. Rev. Melissa Skelton, bishop of the

Diocese of New Westminster in the Anglican Church of Canada
and former rector of St. Paul's in Seattle. "In every parish [that's
discerning a missional move], that conversation needs to happen:
Is this something quite unlike ourselves?" (Skelton).

Mission Past and Present

At the Cathedral Church of St. Paul and the Crossing in Boston,
the missional DNA is about revealing God's reign through radical practices of welcome. And that was present long before the
Rev. Stephanie Spellers's work there or her book, *Radical Welcome*. When the parish became a cathedral in 1912 and the bishop
proclaimed it a "house of prayer for all people," the doors and
the rents came off the box pews. In recent years, those pews have
served as places for street people to rest on cold days, and the welcome extends to Sunday morning. The Very Rev. John (Jep) Streit,
cathedral dean, says St. Paul's "bends over backward to be inclusive" of people with no liturgical background. "Liturgists bristle
at how often we say, 'Now do this, now do that.' But if the people
don't know what they're doing . . ." (Streit). That clarity of mission to the people of the neighborhood laid the groundwork for
the Crossing. Spellers, the Crossing's founder, said her intention
was to create a fresh expression that was true to "our context—
younger, multicultural downtown Boston." Doing so was possible
because the cathedral leadership was "comfortable with the idea
of ministry outside the box—and not just outside the box but truly
reflective of context. They got that" (Spellers).

At the Cathedral of St. John in Denver, the missional DNA
is very different, but the integration between inherited and new
expressions of church works similarly. At St. John's, the core missional identity is about the beauty and transcendence of its worship. That is equally true at the Anglo-Catholic high mass—with
its verger, thurifer, and chanted Gospel proclamation—and at
the Wilderness—with its multitudinous candles, pots of smoking
incense, colorful fabric, and world-music band. In addition to
attracting neighbors, the opulent worship at St. John's is a constant reminder to that *ecclesia* about why the church is there. "'Do

you know God?' That's the longing of all of these people who are looking to the church," said the Rt. Rev. Peter Eaton, bishop of Southeast Florida and former dean of St. John's. Eaton notes that, although churches must be good at process and organizational life, "we have to be very clear about the *reasons* for running the place. Every day, the question has to be, 'What does this have to do with people's relationship with God, and how will it make that deeper?'" (P. Eaton).

Perhaps the clearest link I saw between past and present expressions of missional DNA was at St. Paul's in Richmond, Virginia, and its Center community. At St. Paul's, geography matters. As early as 1897, St. Paul's was offering a "fresh expression" for the businessmen of downtown Richmond—a Lenten series in a local store. That Lenten luncheon continues to this day, along with a number of other ministries to connect with people living and working downtown. What's new about Center is its contemplative nature. Though it's in contrast with St. Paul's usual activist mode of ministry, Center draws on the same impulse that's been driving neighborhood ministry there for more than a century. "Being downtown is really key for us," said the Rev. Wallace Adams-Riley, rector, "and it always has been" (Adams-Riley).

The most explicitly missional congregation I visited was St. Barnabas in London, with its close-up image of running feet above the altar. If a church's destination is to be a community of apostleship, then St. Barnabas is already a long way down the path. But even in that congregation, the Holy Spirit is leading it to express its wiring in new ways and with new populations, sending people to live in community with the poor and raise up a new community of blessing there. St. Barnabas is replicating its missional DNA through Church@Five in Strawberry Vale, empowering people there to see themselves as missionaries to other public-housing communities—and equipping them for that work. "The DNA is exactly the same; it's just expressed differently," said the Rev. Helen Shannon, pastor of Church@Five (who actually describes herself not as a pastor but as "an apostolic prophet") (Shannon).

But a strong missional identity can also be more subtle. At St. James & Emmanuel in Manchester, England, the wiring is about creating generous community, the mustard tree that offers shelter for all sorts of birds of the air. This church of four congregations— from 1662 Holy Communion to contemporary praise and worship to reflective Taize and Iona liturgies—models "unity in diversity" (the nature of the Trinity itself) to its neighbors as an in-breaking of God's reign. It houses local nonprofits, offers its space for hospitality to people in the neighborhood and to asylum-seekers, and offers a youth café in the narthex—intentionally liminal, boundary-crossing space. Expressing that mission in a new way, Abide is working to turn unity into deeper community, equipping people to take their relationships with God and each other more seriously. "The first base within mission is a well-functioning Christian community," said the Rev. Ben Edson, leader of Abide. "So our first goal is to form a community of people, so others find St. James & Emmanuel to be a community they want to belong to" (Edson).

Lessons from the Field

Although congregational leaders may see their church's DNA clearly, most others won't. It may be an issue of not seeing the ecclesial forest for the trees, or it may be that church members have an interest in keeping things the way they are. This may be because of their discomfort with change, investment in inherited interests, or fear of spending resources. So the leadership needs to make the congregation's missional identity as clear as baptismal water. When the Rev. Karen Ward brought her community of seekers together with the faithful remnant of St. Andrew's in Portland, she made her vision plain: a sacramental, Benedictine community that connected with its neighbors to reveal the reign of God. And she left little to individual interpretation. "I put out my vision for the church—how we're going to run things, what's the theology behind it all," she explained. "We did a special retreat, and the Bishop's Advisory Committee approved that vision unanimously. I told them, I'm operating off a four-page document, and I haven't deviated from it one iota. This is what we're doing, and it's all outlined" (Ward).

Even taking more of a work-in-progress approach, people on both ends of the missional process need clarity about who is doing this work and why. In Tewkesbury, England, the Rev. Wendy Ruffle has been intentional about making sure residents of the Prior's Park housing "estate" know their expression of church is connected with the Abbey. The gathering's name on the marketing materials makes it clear: "Celebrate! The Abbey on the Park." The intentionality goes the other way, too. Celebrate! members frequently speak to the Abbey congregation about the ministry and its blessing of them. "I've worked quite hard, actually, at making sure that we remain part of the abbey community," Ruffle said. "Everything I do links back to the abbey" (Ruffle).

It's also important to manifest a common missional identity across inherited and new ministries. At St. Paul's in Seattle, the congregation owns its Anglo-Catholic and Benedictine identity proudly. So Paul Steinke, lay pastor for St. Paul's 5 p.m. Community, has been intentional about shaping that liturgy's practice to reflect the same ethos and then communicating it, particularly to the burned-out evangelicals whom the 5 p.m. Community is reaching. "The 5 p.m. Community is an extension, a part, of that larger identity," Steinke said. The community's worship and common life "helps us understand the breadth of Anglo-Catholic identity and the breadth of Benedictine spirituality, rather than defining it too narrowly—saying, 'It has to look just like this, or it isn't Anglo-Catholic or Benedictine.' What's wonderful about St. Paul's is there's that nuance in the brand" (Steinke).

At Church@5 in London, Shannon also has been intentional about keeping its ministry connected with St. Barnabas without trying to duplicate St. Barnabas in a very different context. "We had to identify our non-negotiables," Shannon said. "What were we going to make sure happened with Church@Five, and what could we just say, 'Because we're small, we can't do that'?" The non-negotiables were culturally relevant worship with modern music, healing prayer, a high doctrine of Scriptural authority, and "eating together, because food poverty is such an issue on the estate." St. Barnabas's ministry clearly manifests those non-negotiables, too (Shannon).

Of course, crystalizing a congregation's missional identity may not be so easy—either because of the complexity of its ministry or, perhaps, because the apostolic energy has been dormant for so long. In that case, look to its founding story or early history. In Denver, the answer was literally in the congregation's original name. Founded during the Colorado gold rush, the church was called St. John's Church in the Wilderness ("About Saint John's Cathedral"), and reaching people in a spiritual wilderness was exactly what the cathedral still felt called to do decades later. Kate Eaton suggests reflecting on questions like these: "'How was our church founded? Who were the founding mothers and fathers? Why did they think of this location? What were the personalities like?' You find little nuggets in that" (K. Eaton). Similarly, the Rev. Paul Williams, vicar of Tewkesbury Abbey, notes that the paradigm for Celebrate! comes out of the abbey's deep history. "This is exactly what the Benedictines did," he said. "As a minster church, the abbey's call was to send and resource medieval church planters. All we've done is just rediscover the minster model" (Williams).

In St. Mary's County, Maryland, the efforts among three congregations to collaborate in new expressions of church tap into strong missional DNA. Ascension, in Lexington Park, was birthed in an iconic location for a parish serving a growing suburb in the 1950s—in a trailer-park laundry. A church doesn't get much more closely connected to people's real lives than that. The congregation also has a strong, enduring identity around serving the poor, housing a food pantry and (in an earlier day) sponsoring a small social-services agency. Ascension, St. George's, and Trinity also serve people outside their walls by bringing them inside, part of a consortium of congregations opening their facilities as homeless shelters during cold months. But in these congregations with colonial backgrounds, the DNA of Christendom and establishment is at least as strong. When the church that began in a laundry built its own worship space a few years later, it put in old box pews removed from a church in Washington, DC. On the bright side, they were half-box pews, without doors on the side aisles. "Episcopalians here got off the boat with the Roman

Catholics 400 years ago," Syler said. "It's 'the church I belong to but don't go to'—very establishment-minded" (Syler).

There's nothing wrong with looking back to find our missional DNA. In fact, we need to. As Williams explained, at Tewkesbury Abbey, "the only way I could talk about mission was to say, 'Within our past, this is what we've done. This is not peculiar; this is what the Benedictines did all through our history.' If the church is caught in its past, it will die. But I have to honor the past and then try to get them to look forward" (Williams).

Indeed, the call to *metanoia*, turning in a God-ward direction, means we can't keep looking back. The boundaries are before us, and we must bring our missional identities to bear on them. True, we can only be who we are. But we can choose to express our most relational and kenotic selves, emulating God's constant moving out in relationship to form relationship, even (and especially) when the cost is high.

References

"About Resurrection." Accessed January 5, 2016. *http://www.cor.org/campus/leawood*.

"About Saint John's Cathedral." Accessed January 5, 2016. *http://www.sjcathedral.org/About*.

Adams-Riley, Wallace. Personal interview by John Spicer. November 5, 2014.

Eaton, Kate. Personal interview 2 by John Spicer. September 20, 2014.

Eaton, Peter. Personal interview by John Spicer. September 20, 2014.

Edson, Ben. Personal interview by John Spicer. May 1, 2014.

Goodhew, David, Andrew Roberts, and Michael Volland. *Fresh! An Introduction to Fresh Expressions of Church and Pioneer Ministry*. London: SCM Press, 2012.

Mobsby, Ian. *God Unknown: The Trinity in Contemporary Spirituality and Mission*. Norwich, UK: Canterbury Press, 2012.

Montgomery, Rick. "Leawood's United Methodist Church of the Resurrection eyes a $90 million overhaul." *Kansas City Star*, March 8, 2014.

Ruffle, Wendy. Personal interview 1 by John Spicer. June 10, 2014.

Shannon, Helen. Personal interview 2 by John Spicer. October 16, 2014.

Skelton, Melissa. Personal interview by John Spicer. September 10, 2014.

Spellers, Stephanie. Personal interview by John Spicer. September 10, 2014.

Steinke, Paul. Personal interview 1 by John Spicer. June 26, 2014.

Streit, John P. Personal interview 2 by John Spicer. September 5, 2014.

Syler, Greg. Personal interview 2 by John Spicer. November 7, 2014.

Ward, Karen. Personal interview 2 by John Spicer. September 30, 2014.

Williams, Paul. Personal interview 1 by John Spicer. July 17, 2014.

4

Whom Are You Trying to Reach—and How?

"[Zacchaeus] ran ahead and climbed a sycamore tree to see [Jesus], because he was going to pass that way. When Jesus came to the place, he looked up and said to him, 'Zacchaeus, hurry and come down; for I must stay at your house today.'"
—Luke 19:4-5

AS A PASTOR AND CONGREGATIONAL LEADER, I find that I have a fondness for theoretical people. They're the people churches tend to plan for. They're tidy. They empty the trash and turn out lights and lock the doors when they leave. They sing during worship. They serve on committees. They pledge as an outward and visible expression of their relationship with the God who loves them.

Unfortunately, as a pastor and congregational leader, I find that what I have are real people. They're messy and cranky sometimes. They may not give a new hymn much of a chance. Some of them serve on one committee after another, and some of them aren't around often enough to pick me out of a lineup. Some of them pledge far more than I would ever ask, and some of them must think magic unicorns pay the church's bills. I love them. And on most days, I like them, too.

If the Gospels tell us anything, they tell us Jesus liked the real ones best. Hypocrites, dullards, casters of stones; the diseased and the rejects; and all sorts of other people as broken as I am. At Christmas, we even remember the stunning, foolhardy truth that in Jesus, God decided to become a real person, too—a sometimes testy, always loving young man who had to deal with followers who consistently missed his point and who skedaddled when the authorities turned against him. The mystery of the Incarnation is perhaps most fully expressed in the fact that he loved them anyway—and then sent them out to be his "witnesses in Jerusalem, in all Judea and Samaria, and to the ends of the earth" (Acts 1:8).

In medieval England, when the priest and villagers would go to the ends of their parish and beat the bounds, I imagine one of the great benefits was the chance to see and talk with the real people at the edge of the villagers' experience. I love the image of people from one parish lining up on their side of a boundary stream while people from the next parish lined up opposite them, someone tossing over a rope, and the two parishes playing tug of war (Stilgoe 50). (Presumably the villagers who *weren't* beating the bounds had the stronger team, since their youngsters hadn't recently been slammed into trees or dunked into water.) You get to know people when they tug you past your boundary, or you tug them past theirs, and someone ends up in the stream, head first.

Trying to reach people at the edges of our church boundaries feels less like a tug of war and more like trying to push a rope. The people on the other end of our missional efforts have to do very little to frustrate our best intentions. All they need to do is . . . nothing—especially when they're theoretical people, those lovely folks who *excel* at doing nothing. They're particularly good at doing nothing I want them to do, like coming to new and interesting worship services.

Clergy and laypeople in the Church of England have been working on fresh expressions of church for more than a decade now, and their online fresh expressions guide offers a bevy of good, practical suggestions for incarnating the missional strands congregations find in their DNA. One of the guide's clearest directions is about getting started. The key operational question isn't, "What should we offer?" or "What will attract (theoretical) people who aren't here?" Instead comes the incarnational question, the search for real people: "Whom is the Spirit leading us to serve?" The fresh expressions guide offers this advice: "Midwives of church must think people, not models. Often they know that church must be different but have only half the story. . . . The Spirit takes you beyond your initial understanding that church must be different, to seeing how church can be different for people you are called to serve. Your imagination expands from 'this is how church could be fresh' to 'this is how it could be fresh *for them* (or *for us*)'" ("How Should We Start?").

That question—whom is the Spirit leading us to serve?—came before all the congregations I studied. Some engaged it quite explicitly, some more implicitly, some less directly than would have been helpful, in hindsight. Sooner or later, every congregation seeking to beat its boundaries has to ask, "Whom are we trying to reach—and how?" And it's better to ask sooner than later.

Look Nearby

At the Crossing in Boston, the "who" came from the congregation's commitment to the neighborhood, a commitment St. Paul's had incarnated for decades. The Rev. Stephanie Spellers identified the need to extend the cathedral's radical welcome to the multicultural students and young professionals in downtown—people who passed by St. Paul's each day as they walked to work or jogged in Boston Common. Spellers was trained as a community organizer, and she wondered what would happen if she applied those principles in the context of downtown Boston to start a new congregation. "What if you went out listening and asked people what drives them—'If you could start fresh Christian community, given the city we live in, given the particular local context, what would be happening?'" (Spellers). For Spellers, that process was about building community first and letting the marks of church rise from those relationships. She started meeting with people who were simply exploring spirituality, learning their interests and values, and building a network. "They began gathering in each other's homes, eating together, getting to know each other, and dreaming together," said Isaac Everett, the Crossing's minister of liturgical arts. "It took about six months for that process to happen" before they had their first worship (Everett).

In Richmond, the "who" was also a function of location because of St. Paul's long history of ministry to downtown. In creating Center as part of downtown mission, the Rev. Melanie Mullen also took a community-organizing approach in reaching out to downtown residents and workers—from homeless people to hipsters to loft dwellers to state bureaucrats. She networked with parishioners who gave her contacts, and Mullen brought them together for listening sessions to find out "what their lives are like—what needs they have, what they're looking for in terms of community and relationship—as well as their comfort level with the church," she said (Mullen, Personal interview 1). From that process, she heard two oddly juxtaposed desires: connection and retreat. Although people talked about their loneliness and need for community, they also craved space for personal connection with the divine: "People clearly said, 'I want to feel like I'm unobserved at times.' They needed some cloistered, private space; they wanted to be in sacred darkness" (Mullen, Personal interview 2).

The geographic sense of "parish" helps define the "who" for St. Andrew and All Souls (SAAS) in Portland. On one level, says the Rev. Karen Ward, the parish is the entire "fifth quadrant" of north Portland—but 50,000 people are fairly theoretical. SAAS knows its identity clearly: a progressive, welcoming, sacramental, Benedictine community in a working-class, culturally diverse neighborhood. That SAAS ethos seems to connect especially with former Roman Catholics, former evangelicals, LGBTQ people, and those who connect spirituality with the arts. The experience of member Justin Morgan represents real people of north Portland for whom SAAS can be a haven. Raised in "a fairly austere fundamentalist evangelical home," Morgan later worshiped in Vineyard and Mennonite churches and lived in an intentional community. But when he came out as gay, he felt ostracized, had a crisis of faith, and left church entirely. He couldn't take the kind of preaching he'd known, but he felt himself drawn to liturgical worship: "The language that I was open to was the language of art, ritual, chant, incense, and candles—the language of symbols," he said. "Writing icons became a way for me to connect to the divine without having to articulate anything with my mind. So, icons specifically and traditional liturgy in general was my pathway back to connecting to my faith" (Morgan). Morgan's icons now adorn the SAAS nave, speaking to pilgrims on a similar path.

In Seattle, St. Paul's sense of "who" is less about geography and more about groups. Initially, St. Paul's thought its 5 p.m. Community would reach younger people, especially those without children; former Roman Catholics; and the LGBTQ seekers who had been coming to St. Paul's for some time. "But I'd been there long enough to realize who we thought we would reach and who actually shows up might be two different things," said the Rt. Rev. Melissa Skelton, former rector (Skelton). In addition to the groups St. Paul's had targeted, young evangelicals became a large proportion of the 5 p.m. Community, both because of the connections lay pastor Paul Steinke brought from the Seattle School of Theology and Psychology and because of the longstanding "symbiosis" between St. Paul's and Seattle Pacific University, said Mark Taylor, former senior warden (Taylor). The young evangelicals were "looking for a way to stay in a church, looking for something a little more improvisational, a different manifestation of intimacy in community life" than what they'd known before, Skelton explained (Skelton).

In Tewkesbury and London, the real people church leaders had in mind were those struggling with poverty in nearby public-housing "estates"—though different motivations spurred the congregations' efforts. Tewkesbury Abbey built a community in Prior's Park because of the abbey's call to serve its geographic parish—all of it. "We reached out to the poor because that happens to be the context that the Abbey's placed within," said the Rev. Wendy Ruffle. "Paul [Williams, the vicar] recognized the Abbey had a gap in Prior's Park. Folk from Prior's Park had always wanted to bring their children to be baptized, and a few would get married in the Abbey, but not many. So Paul had an inspired idea of sending somebody into Prior's Park to gather families together" (Ruffle, Personal interview 1). At St. Barnabas in London, the call was more directly about serving poor people; and the Strawberry

Vale housing estate provided an opportunity relatively close by. St. Barnabas bought a house on the estate so the Rev. Helen Shannon could move in and build a community of relationships, one real person at a time. She and volunteers put in more than a year of that work before worship ever happened.

In Denver, leaders took the opposite approach, developing worship before trying to build community. They too had a group in mind—initially hikers, skiers, and others with Sunday morning conflicts. With more discernment, the focus shifted to the "tattooed, kind of angry, Goth-looking crowd" near the cathedral, said liturgy planner Kate Eaton (Eaton). Later, that target group broadened in terms of age and lifestyle but also became more focused: people seeking anonymity and safety in connecting with God. "This service is meant to call to people who basically would never set foot in a church, people who don't have the background," said Priscilla Shand, part of the Wilderness set-up team (Shand). Wilderness worshiper and cathedral vestry member Suni Devitt agrees: "The purpose is to connect with people who haven't yet figured out what they're looking for. The service is dark; you can come in and listen, and you can leave whenever" (Devitt).

Identifying the "who" was one of the stumbling blocks for the three congregations in St. Mary's County, Maryland. In developing Gather Eat Pray, leaders agreed they were targeting young adults and families. They narrowed it further to what the Rev. Greg Syler called "liturgical Christians who are not drawn to more contemporary expressions of worship, but who need something besides historical cemeteries and churches" (Syler). Young adults and families in the congregations led the effort, people who themselves wanted a new expression of worship—seemingly a healthy sign. But that expression ended after a year primarily because its leaders had different visions of how the community should worship (as well as facing programming challenges with children of wide-ranging ages). Those different visions reflected the leaders' personal preferences; they hadn't come to consensus on how to reach people because they weren't sure whom they were trying to reach, other than people like each of them. Of course, different individual preferences came out as disagreements about worship gatherings because each was trying to connect with theoretical people "like me."

Lessons from the Field

Connecting with real people starts by making peace with this "new normal" of congregational life: Developing the new expressions of church that God desires isn't a quick—or a programmatic—process. It's long, slow, slogging work with one individual after another, and it's nothing new. Building the *ecclesia* has been like this from the start, as true in the first apostolic age as in the present one. Apostles' "primary gift is to fit human relationships together," regardless of the time in which they serve (Goodhew, Roberts, and Volland 17). But between those apostolic ages, the Church became comfortable relying on its privileged position in society and the power (often brutality) it could wield in missionary work. Even fifty years ago, we could simply open mainline congregations in new neighborhoods, and the neighbors would show up. This allowed the Church to substitute amnesia for anamnesis, forgetting that Jesus comes to be present in the midst of particular human beings. That forgetting—our reliance on institutional muscle or the denominational brand—was Christendom's disruption of Christianity's larger pattern of taking individuals seriously.

For Spellers at the Crossing in Boston, the mission was to identify neighborhood people who felt alienated from church. Practically, that meant finding some. So Spellers and her team identified friends who weren't involved in church, only attended occasionally, or whose children had dropped out. "We looked around and we listened," Spellers said. "Every time we finished a conversation, we'd ask, 'Is there anyone else you know who has these questions or shares your passions? Can I talk with that person?'" (Spellers).

Identifying "who" also involves showing up consistently in places where relationships can grow naturally. Spellers makes a practice of going to the same bar once a week. "They know I'm a priest; and when I sit down, people just come up," she said. "It opens up all kinds of conversations." Rather than moving among locations and approaching people cold, Spellers advises consistency. "Go to a bar or coffeehouse and be present, be incarnate," she said. "Sit at your table, hang out, and listen. Eventually, the people who work there will get to know you. Eventually, you'll have conversations" (Spellers). She cautions there are no shortcuts to this kind of listening process; just becoming known takes at least six months. Mullen, who studied with Spellers, spends a lot of her time "one-on-one-ing" the people she meets through downtown Richmond activities. "The only kind of power you have is to tap your connections with other people," Mullen said (Mullen, Personal interview 2).

From those kinds of connections, modern-day apostles can then get involved in the things that matter to the people they're trying to reach. "It's easier if the people you're seeking see you doing the things they're doing," Spellers explained. "Don't put on funky worship; host an event for yoga people shaped by what the yoga people want to do. Watch them, come alongside them, be of service to them. Then you have opportunities for collaboration that don't feel artificial and creepy" (Spellers).

The relational investment needs to be intensive, sustained, and oriented toward people's well-being rather than the congregation's interest, which is perhaps the most countercultural aspect of new expressions of ministry. In Tewkesbury, Ruffle said she went into her work in Prior's Park expecting to invest a year in relationship-building—"tramping around the community"—before creating anything programmatic. She was shocked that the Holy Spirit inspired her to create the first gathering of what became Celebrate! after just a few months. "It's about looking at the context, seeing what the need is within this context, and then reaching and blessing the folk," Ruffle explained (Ruffle, Personal interview 2).

Of course, what that blessing looks like varies from context to context, as does the extent to which it manifests itself as something spiritual, something formational, or something that meets day-to-day needs. In contexts of poverty, both Ruffle and Shannon included food with fellowship early on in reaching people on housing "estates." In Boston, Spellers brought together her core connections for "worship learning parties" to try out corporate prayer that addressed people's needs—church practiced with authenticity, relationship, and connection with ancient tradition. From those events, she invited attendees to help her build the kind of community the worship enfleshed. "That's what organizers do," she said. "They use action to generate more leadership, to give people the chance to become leaders and experience a community around a common purpose. Then you just keep building experiences, and pretty soon you have a group of people ready to *be* church, not just go to church" (Spellers). In Richmond, Mullen and her team heard a call to provide space for spiritual reflection—but what to offer, and when, was much more art than science. Though Mullen didn't want to create a worship service and hope people would come, the neighborhood need she discerned called for at least a quasi-liturgical response.

Again, the focus is what matters: on "them," not on the church. That's true in the sense of following a missional motivation that puts real people's needs ahead of the congregation's desire to grow. It's also true in the sense of how to incarnate that mission, even when the motivation is comparatively selfless. At Tewkesbury Abbey, Ruffle's mission to Prior's Park wasn't the abbey's first attempt to serve people there. Before, "I think we were trying to take the abbey's culture out into these areas," explained the Rev. Paul Williams, abbey vicar. "The expectation that if you put something on, people will come to it—it just doesn't work. You've got to create a hook onto the culture—find out why people are going to a particular place and how you can work into that" (Williams).

And yet, it's still tempting to put something on and hope theoretical people will come to it. Maybe we need to try that to present an experiential challenge to our inherited wiring. Not surprisingly, even people who write books aren't immune from the temptation to try something that aligns more with institutional than missional church, hoping there might be enough gas left in the tank to make the trip worthwhile. Here's a case study, perhaps a cautionary tale, from my congregation, St. Andrew's in Kansas City.

In 2013, we launched a Saturday evening service called Take 5. The idea was to meet an expressed need in the congregation and, we hoped, connect with people in our neighborhood who weren't attracted to our fairly typical Sunday morning Rite I and Rite II liturgies. Internally, a number of younger parishioners, several with families, were asking for a casual, shorter celebration of Holy Eucharist with more accessible and contemporary music. They specifically said late Saturday afternoon would be most convenient for them and other younger adults they knew. The service started off with forty to fifty people coming, and our newly called, late-twenties priest, the Rev. Marcus Halley, was the principal presider.

Even while the attendance continued to be in the forties, we recognized that few of the people who had asked for the liturgy actually attended, and neither did their contemporaries from the neighborhood. Instead, the attendees were parishioners across age groups for whom the service time, length, or style met a need. Once the newness wore off, attendance began slipping; and the clergy and music director agreed a compelling style had never really gelled. So about eighteen months after its launch, we began retooling. Informal worship with praise music hadn't seemed to be a good fit, so we went in a different direction. We kept the service length at less than an hour, but we changed the music to a small, quasi-professional choral group accompanied by organ (seeking something like an English evensong vibe); we made the homily short and reflective, leaving people with questions with which to wrestle; and we offered three prayer stations—with candles, incense, icons, and participatory activities—to serve as Prayers of the People. We also moved the service from Saturday to Sunday evening, largely because of conflicts with Saturday weddings. The new service, Ascend, also drew curious parishioners at first, as well as a few new faces from the neighborhood. Then its attendance began dropping, too.

Take 5 and Ascend illustrate the risk of programming for hypothetical people "out there." With Take 5, we did listen to real people in the parish, hearing what they wanted and what they were hearing from their contemporaries—but the service was less viable than we'd hoped. With Ascend, we talked with people attending Take 5 to get their feedback on retooling the service. But in neither case did we go beyond our boundaries to talk to real people around us.

I think we'll do things differently next time.

References

Devitt, Suni. Personal interview by John Spicer. September 21, 2014.

Eaton, Kate. Personal interview 1 by John Spicer. June 2, 2014.

Everett, Isaac. Personal interview 1 by John Spicer. May 8, 2014.

Goodhew, David, Andrew Roberts, and Michael Volland. *Fresh! An Introduction to Fresh Expressions of Church and Pioneer Ministry.* London: SCM Press, 2012.

"How Should We Start?" Accessed January 7, 2016. *http://www.fresh expressions.org.uk/guide/starting/how.*

Morgan, Justin. E-mail correspondence with John Spicer. September 30, 2014.

Mullen, Melanie. Personal interview 1 by John Spicer. April 3, 2014.

———. Personal interview 2 by John Spicer. November 3, 2014.

Ruffle, Wendy. Personal interview 1 by John Spicer. June 10, 2014.

———. Personal interview 2 by John Spicer. October 10, 2014.

Shand, Priscilla. Personal interview by John Spicer. September 19, 2014.

Skelton, Melissa. Personal interview by John Spicer. September 10, 2014.

Spellers, Stephanie. Personal interview by John Spicer. September 10, 2014.

Stilgoe, John R. "Jack-O'-Lanterns to Surveyors: The Secularization of Landscape Boundaries." In *Landscape and Images*, 47–63. Charlottesville: University of Virginia Press, 2005.

Syler, Greg. E-mail correspondence 1 with John Spicer. April 10, 2014.

Taylor, Mark. Personal interview by John Spicer. October 3, 2014.

Williams, Paul. Personal interview 1 by John Spicer. July 17, 2014.

5

What Expression of Ministry Is God Trying to Create?

"Let us rejoice and exult and give [God] the glory, for the marriage of the Lamb has come. . . . Blessed are those who are invited to the marriage supper of the Lamb."
—Revelation 19:7, 9

THIS ISN'T COOL, BUT I HAVE TO SAY THAT I'm fond of Rite I and Rite II liturgies on Sunday morning. Granted, any given week, they may not set your feet to tapping or break open God's Word in a way that connects directly with your heart—or they may. But you can rely on this: No matter where you are, you'll find comfortable words (even if Rite I's Comfortable Words are omitted) and the body and blood of Christ. I remember, as a boy, traveling with my family every summer to visit my grandparents in California. My mother would take my sisters and me to the Episcopal congregation in Delano, a congregation where we didn't know a soul. But we weren't intimidated because we could bank on finding Holy Communion according to the Book of Common Prayer, as well as songs from the hymnal. I marveled at the reality that I could go to "my" church even thousands of miles away from home. And I have to admit that I carry that experience into my priesthood. As much as I enjoy alternative liturgies (and I really do), I find myself "at home" with Rite I and Rite II on Sunday morning. So I empathize with my parishioners who tell me (the priest who changes

things too much) that, on Sunday morning, they just want to hear
those comfortable words.

Good old Rite I and Rite II Sunday morning liturgies are like
Shady Inn, the "classy" steak house I grew up visiting in Springfield, Missouri. When my grandparents made the trek from California to come see us, the visit always included a meal at Shady
Inn. You knew what was waiting for you: a white tablecloth; a
cornucopia of crackers and real butter; a round of cocktails before
dinner (including Shirley Temples for the kids); iceberg lettuce
salads; and finally six choices of steak. My mother was the radical because she got shish kebab (which meant the steak was in
chunks and was dangerously near vegetables), and it came with
rice instead of potato. We didn't understand her. How could you
go wrong with steak and potatoes at Shady Inn?

Today, the Episcopal congregation in Delano, California, and
Shady Inn both are closed. Although many of us are still fans, it
turns out not everyone wants steak and potatoes.

Those of us who find traditional worship predictably satisfy-
ing may understand, intellectually, that we can't just offer more
slight variations on a theme—the church's equivalent of six cuts
of steak. But for many of us, the wiring and the habit run deep. If
our congregations want to grow (either because of our desire to
share good news or our anxiety about declining pledge income),
our options often begin with tweaking worship or offering services
at different times, as my congregation has tried with an evening
liturgy. Too often, our options also end there.

To push the analogy probably too far: Not only are people no
longer just looking for a good steak-and-potato dinner; these days,
many aren't even looking for a restaurant. And congregations
are learning that they need to provide rich nourishment—"true
bread," in fact—in new ways.

From Ian Mobsby's perspective, it's about time. The founder
of Moot in London began his new monastic community in a parish church, St. Matthew's, Westminster, in London. It started as
a discussion group but found its heart as an intentional community seeking to reach the spiritual-but-not-religious. "We built a
community from the de-churched to reach out to the unchurched,"

Mobsby said (Mobsby). Today, at St. Mary Aldermary church in central London, where Moot is housed, you can stop in to enjoy an excellent coffee, a lovely scone, several discussion opportunities, art displays . . . oh, and worship happens there daily, too. So if the coffee and conversation have hooked your heart, you're welcome to stay and pray with the community, bread and wine included.

The order matters. "Be really careful that you don't overplay worship," Mobsby said. "You're not going to reach the unchurched if you're using the medium of engagement of worship. The best you're going to do is reach some open de-churched, but you'll never get the unchurched. I think the church is slightly addicted to worship services" (Mobsby).

Instead, at Moot, the coffee is the sacramental connection. There in London's financial district, Mobsby explained, the culture's values come through in high relief. "This is a place of such greed and anger—horrible things in the name of work," he said. "But an amazing thing is going on [at Moot and its café] because it doesn't fit at all with the values of the area. Here's a bunch of poor hipsters trying to reach out to a load of rich, very posh, people, many of whom are depressed. It's the poor reaching out to the very rich, which has got to be the essence of the kingdom of God" (Mobsby).

To beat the boundaries of our congregations and our own hearts—to offer people true bread in new ways—we need to have more than worship on the menu, and it probably shouldn't be the first course. In our faithful interaction with the folks we find at our boundaries, the Holy Spirit goes to work—work that plays out differently context by context. But we have to engage the question: What expression of ministry is God trying to create?

It's a lesson the English church has learned through the fresh expressions movement, encouraging new forms of church to rise up in the midst of established Anglicanism. The *Mission-Shaped Church* report calls the process "double listening"—"listening to the culture where a church might be established, and to the inherited tradition of the gospel and the church." Listening to the world comes first because it shapes what emerges. "Then the second aspect of double listening validates it, through connection of the faith uniquely revealed in the Scriptures" and two thousand years of church tradition. And continuing the double-listening process as the ministry goes on "enables something to evolve as its context changes" (Archbishop's Council on Mission and Public Affairs 104–105).

The congregations I visited took different paths to create something new, some more process-oriented and some following the Sprit's lead more intuitively. But each is bearing fruit, though some is riper than others.

What Are You Building?

The Crossing in Boston sees its work as nothing less than creating a community of disciples, alongside the ministries of St. Paul's Cathedral, in order to change the world. Liturgical arts minister Isaac Everett hears that call as the antidote to contemporary spiritual maladies. "I see more and more loneliness, apathy, and cynicism taking over our culture, certainly among my age peers [20s and 30s]," he said. "Religious community and spiritual practice is the best medicine for that that I know. People are just deeply thirsty for hope, for love, and for belief that it's possible to change the world. That's what I think the Crossing is doing" (Everett).

Everett and Crossing members have built that community—and continue to build it—by developing relationships one coffee at a time and intentionally connecting people into the Crossing's life. It's made the Crossing "not just a service but a gathering of friends," explained Annie Kurdzeil, a three-year member. Although engagement with a church can become centered on members' relationships with clergy (especially the rector/senior pastor), what matters more are the relationships among the folks. "You need that web," she said. "You touch these people, and they touch other people, and community just kind of comes into existence" (Kurdzeil).

As a result, the Crossing has become church for its members, not a ministry of an institution—a parallel congregation rather than a cathedral service (some Crossing members aren't aware of the cathedral at all). And membership means much more than appearing on a parish register and attending worship three times a year. "Very few people have *not* been involved in some leadership or group experience," Kurdzeil said. "We're probably not the community for someone who just wants to sit on the outside" (Kurdzeil).

At St. Paul's in Richmond, the Rev. Melanie Mullen uses the same community-development approach to build relationships that build church. But Center isn't intended to create a parallel congregation any more than St. Paul's other manifestations of downtown mission, such as block parties, "ashes to go" on Ash Wednesday, and music and poetry nights at a coffeehouse in nearby Shockoe Bottom. Instead, Center does what St. Paul's does but in what Mullen calls a "left-handed" way, creating space for contemplative engagement with God as well as tight community. She heard those needs expressed directly from people the ministry would serve. She networked with parishioners who referred her to people they knew downtown. She and the rest of the planning team invited contacts they'd made to come for listening sessions so they could hear about the needs and desires of those contacts. They offered test worship—from open-space contemplative time in St. Paul's to new liturgies in other locations—and listened to feedback. What they heard was a desire both for individual connection with God and corporate connection as community. Center meets those vertical and horizontal needs through contemplative worship, discussion, and a meal.

At St. Andrew and All Souls (SAAS) in Portland, the model preceded the people, but it's tailored to the parish's context. In a sense, the Rev. Karen Ward is creating something very similar to what she built at Church of the Apostles (COTA) in Seattle— worship that's "ancient, sacramental, contemplative, culturally resonate and creative" ("FAQ") in a "neo-Benedictine" environment involving daily prayer, Scripture reflection, attentiveness to building community, Holy Eucharist, contemplation, and retreat" ("Spirituality"). She strongly encourages parishioners to adopt a rule of life and commit to daily spiritual practice. "I did the same thing at COTA; it's no different from what I did there," she said, but the context determines how it plays out. At SAAS, the missional ethos is about connecting with its neighbors through feeding and hospitality, and all its ministries point that direction. Whether expressed in worship, arts programs, a café, or a food pantry, "it's about feeding people's need for spirituality, community, and sustenance," Ward said. "Through that, we can access anybody in the neighborhood—from the atheist who comes in to get a latte at the café, to the anarchist kid who plays music at a concert, to the poor person who comes in to get a bag of groceries. It's all feeding; it's all welcoming" (Ward). And that applies equally to a standard Rite II Sunday morning Eucharist, which Ward plans to reinstate when resources allow.

In Manchester, England, the Rev. Ben Edson is forming a community within the parish church explicitly to change that church—"working within the institution toward being a renewal of the institution," he said (Edson). Abide is "the missional community" of St. James & Emmanuel, but its shape isn't what you might expect. Rather than focusing on proclamation or service or even relationship-building beyond the church walls, Abide is more like an intentional community with very porous boundaries. Abide invites its participants to adopt a rule of life remarkably similar to the Episcopal Baptismal Covenant—the Five Rhythms of Grace—but no formal profession of affiliation is required ("The Five Rhythms of Grace"). Abide gathers twice a month, once in the context of the existing Sunday evening service at Emmanuel and again for a community dinner—but both gatherings are open to anyone. By asking its members to live intentionally as Christians through spiritual practices, and by building a strong community that breaks bread and shares their hearts, Abide is sowing missional seeds rather than organizing mission-related programs. The intent is to form individual hearts first, then let the Holy Spirit choose which particular boundaries those individuals might engage. "For me, cultivating a sense of 'be' is as important as cultivating a sense of mission," said member Beth Dickinson (Dickinson).

While Abide is the newest expression of church at St. James & Emmanuel, the Rev. Nick Bundock argues that longer-term, more traditional ministries help it beat its boundaries just as much. Emmanuel's parish center, built in 2007, is a conduit to the community, bringing in neighbors for parties and receptions, families for dance classes, and groups for meetings—as well as asylum seekers needing shelter from the storm. The parish's school has been a connecting point with the community for four hundred years, and high demand has led the church to open a second school about a mile from Emmanuel. "I find the boundaries of fresh expressions to be really blurred," Bundock said. "We're opening a new church school to serve a new community, with our ministry at the heart of it. To me, that's a fresh expression" (Bundock).

In Seattle, St. Paul's created the 5 p.m. Community as a new service to keep the congregation growing. Through a collaborative development process, St. Paul's built an improvisational expression of the congregation's core Anglo-Catholic and Benedictine spirituality, finding freedom within the tradition's boundaries. Its developers were careful to make the 5 p.m. worship feel like St. Paul's while bringing a new expression of St. Paul's to the table, differentiating its worship life especially through shared preaching and art as proclamation of the Word. And recognizing the new liturgy's appeal to younger people leaving charismatic evangelical traditions, the Rt. Rev. Melissa Skelton, former rector, brought in someone to lead the 5 p.m. Community, Paul Steinke, who could speak their language and relate to their experience.

The Wilderness in Denver began entirely as worship, with no particular intention of gathering people for further fellowship or formation. The goal was to create a liturgy very different from Sunday morning's inherited forms but true to the beauty, sacramentality, and rich sensory experience of the Anglo-Catholic tradition. The Rt. Rev. Peter Eaton, the former dean of the cathedral where the Wilderness is located, explained that he had certain parameters for the new liturgy, but he stayed out of its development to allow the creativity of others to carry the day. "I said it had to be Eucharist every week, because if the unchurched want mystery and a deeper relationship with God, then it's the sacramental system we need to find a way to make available to them," he explained. Eaton also required that the service use new liturgical texts so it would "be a crucible for newer ventures in expansive language and form." Finally, and perhaps counterintuitively, he specified that its design not be age specific ("this was not to be a twenties and thirties event") and that cathedral clergy share the presiding and preaching roles so that the liturgy wouldn't become personality focused. "As a consequence, the Wilderness is still going nine years later, after three changes in pastoral leadership," Eaton noted (P. Eaton).

The Wilderness continues to bring in people at the boundaries of the cathedral's inherited life. Its dark, anonymous worship attracts about sixty people on a Sunday evening—safe and sacred space with no strings attached. Over time, cathedral leaders have also tried to build community out of the worship experience, but they've met challenges along the way. For several years, worshipers were invited to a local watering hole for food, drink, and conversation—and about ten people would usually take part. Now, Sunday nights include dinner at the cathedral and a formation opportunity—though the socioeconomic mix, homeless people gathering with soccer moms, presents its own challenges. The cathedral is finding that compelling worship may draw in de-churched people, but it often doesn't encourage them to stay. The Rev. Jadon Hartsuff, who oversees the Wilderness, says their formational and pastoral needs are just as strong—or stronger. "Many people who've fallen away from the church are actually more hungry for care and community—for conversation at an inclusive and intelligent level—than they are for worship," he explained. "This idea people will flock to the church because it presents some different worship experience—that was true here to an extent, but many didn't stay. They didn't deepen their life spiritually or in the community of the cathedral; they've come and gone" (Hartsuff).

In Tewkesbury and London, building community was key to their efforts to plant new expressions in contexts of poverty and social difference, taking Tewkesbury Abbey and St. Barnabas directly to disadvantaged people. Though the planting congregations are about as different as you can imagine in churchmanship, they followed a remarkably similar process that created remarkably similar expressions of church. Both began with deeply incarnational pastoral investment, sending a priest to live and work on a housing "estate," get involved in the community, watch for the

Holy Spirit's work already underway, and discern how to increase God's blessing there. Both efforts took real people, and their needs, very seriously, always offering food as part of gatherings and pastoral presence virtually 24/7. Both Celebrate! and Church@Five emphasize doing church *with* people rather than *for* people. Both expressions of worship get estate residents actively involved in proclamation—through Bible study and discussion at Church@ Five, and through crafts and drama at Celebrate!. Both plants are intentionally striking a balance between autonomy and connection with their sending congregations; as the Rev. Wendy Ruffle said, Celebrate! is a bridge between the abbey and Prior's Park, a congregation with its own integrity and leadership but also "the abbey on the Park" (Ruffle). Interestingly, both services offer Eucharist only occasionally (even the plant from the Anglo-Catholic abbey) because the leaders feel Church of England requirements for receiving Eucharist create a boundary that reinforces disadvantaged people's sense of difference and exclusion. But in honoring people's embodiment, creating worship that involves the senses richly, and practicing a radical commitment of presence in the estates, both Celebrate! and Church@Five are deeply sacramental expressions of church. As the Rev. Paul Williams, abbey vicar, put it, all worship at Celebrate! is eucharistic "because to have people gathered around a table is really inclusive, and a majority of these people live lives in which they're quite often excluded from the table" (Williams, Personal interview 1).

At St. George's, Ascension, and Trinity parishes in St. Mary's County, Maryland, leaders have also been addressing unintentional exclusion, boundaries created both by box pews and social expectations. But just as challenging have been the boundaries that arise between congregations, reinforced by Episcopal Church polity, tradition, and congregational pride. Though Gather Eat Pray and Thirsty Theology have tried to open doors of worship, formation, and fellowship for people in the community, the freshest expression of ministry there has been the congregations' work to create a level of governance to coordinate shared ministries and manage their costs. (See chapter 6, p. 118.)

Lessons from the Field

As St. Paul reminds us, "If anyone is in Christ, there is a new creation" (2 Cor. 5:17); so in discerning what new expression of ministry God is trying to create, remember that each divine creation must have its own integrity. Taking someone else's cool, successful expression of ministry and trying to replicate it is just as top-down as the inherited model of planting an English parish in Delano, California. "The last thing to do is to look at the Crossing, or any emerging form of church, and try to copy what they're doing," said Mary Beth Mills-Curran, a five-year Crossing member. "Instead, assemble the people you've gathered and say, 'What would worship say about us and what we believe?'" (Mills-Curran).

The process of double listening isn't easy. Even an individual's work to discern God's call isn't necessarily linear, and it certainly doesn't align neatly with ecclesial structures and timelines. So, with a listening process involving multiple leaders and attempting to match congregational DNA with the lives of real people beyond the church's boundaries, expect a longer timeline than will make anyone comfortable. In my parish, St. Andrew's in Kansas City, we've made some progress but certainly with stumbling steps. In late 2013, we created a new clergy position to lead our efforts to reach people in new ways, and we called the Rev. Marcus Halley as pastor for young adults and families. His focus was to be that demographic among existing parishioners and beyond. In hindsight, based on the experience of other places I visited, this demographic focus probably reflected congregational anxiety about the future at least as much as getting on board with the Holy Spirit's work. In addition, the need for collaboration among our formation ministries, as well as Halley's passion for catechumenal formation, led me to make adult formation part of his portfolio; and his responsibility for reaching new people in new ways brought marketing under his purview, too. It seems "mission creep" isn't limited to military operations. Halley's work would have been slow in any event, given its relational nature, but the expansion of responsibility didn't help. Or maybe it did—allowing the Holy Spirit to work in ways we weren't expecting. Energizing the inquirer's process and creating a catechumenal program led to a group of more than a dozen adults preparing for baptism, confirmation, reception into the church, or reaffirmation of baptismal vows. That's up from, um, zero, previously. And, by the way, eight of the dozen were under forty.

In addition, the double-listening process for a new expression of ministry also has been moving along, though (again) at a slower pace than my anxiety would prefer. Fairly soon after coming to St. Andrew's, Halley began spending time hanging out in coffeehouses, hoping connections would happen. Not many did. Apparently, community development isn't as simple as, "If you drink it, they will come." Based on input from other places I visited, we probably didn't stick with that process long enough or work it hard enough for it to bear fruit. But through a range of interactions less intentional than I might have scripted—including work with the interfaith community in Kansas City, efforts to fight racism locally, and simply the practice of parish ministry with existing members—Halley's work has helped us see a way we might match St. Andrew's gifts with the needs of real people the Holy Spirit has brought into our orbit: the intersection of arts and spirituality. How that will play out is a work in progress, with a small group (existing members and newcomers) exploring it together. What I know is this: St. Andrew's membership, attendance, and pledging have been holding steady; formation ministries are growing; and we're doing a better job of helping visitors explore a journey toward membership. I wish the process of creating new expressions of ministry was straight and clear; I'd certainly sleep better if it were. But it's not.

That being said, the congregations I visited offer some helpful insights in working with the Holy Spirit to raise up new creations and beat our boundaries. Probably most important is the need to invest in the long, slow, slogging work of what Mullen calls "one-on-oneing people" (Mullen). That community-organizing technique is the backbone of Mullen's work in Richmond and the staying power of the Crossing in Boston. The work begins with the proverbial cup of coffee, but that's just the start. From one conversation come connections with that person's network, and a web of relationships comes into being. And the organizer keeps the conversations going, coming back to his or her connections once they're on board with a ministry, holding them accountable, encouraging them to take a next step and reach someone else. "Most of the entrepreneurial ministry people I know, they've all done community-organizing training," Mullen said. "No one has any other idea of a process" to build new communities (Mullen).

Alongside that truth is the chicken-and-egg dynamic of forming community vs. offering something into which to invite people. At one end of the spectrum is the Crossing's approach, building community and seeing what worship, formation, and service springs from it; at the other end is the Wilderness, offering worship and taking pains not to pressure anonymous attendees into anything more. Clearly, there is no right answer, and any approach will have its benefits and costs. As Mobsby observes, worship will only attract the open de-churched, people with some experience in a spiritual community who are willing to take a chance on something new. In the Wilderness's experience, the high quality of the worship has kept the numbers up—at sixty or so, the best-attended new expression I visited. But Wilderness leaders have struggled to build community from that experience, trying to keep the service from being a revolving door. A tighter-knit community, begun through intentional organizing, has the potential for a rich corporate life of worship, formation, and blessing to the larger community around it—but the numbers seem destined to remain smaller. Not surprisingly, the best answer is the one that fits the context. For Ward in Portland, echoing the book *Liquid Church*,[1] effective new ministry is "like water moving though a rock," she said. "If it finds a hole or a crack, it goes in and keeps moving. So there's no model other than you find where there's a crack and the water can get in. You just try to make an opening and go through it" (Ward).

Whatever route the liquid takes, it needs to reflect a baptismal ecclesiology. Clergy (myself included) are notorious for advocating the ministry of the baptized when it comes to chairing committees or running pledge campaigns, but the test comes with ministries more

---

1. Pete Ward, *Liquid Church* (Peabody, MA: Hendrickson Publishers, 2002).

traditionally in the clerical domain—like preaching. A willingness to let others break open God's Word is part of the emerging church ethos, and it can play out in many ways. At the Crossing, lay preaching was part of the Rev. Stephanie Spellers's intent from the beginning, leading her not to preach at the Crossing for its first three years. Shared preaching is also a hallmark of life at SAAS in Portland, where proclamation might take the form of original poetry or music, small group conversations, a guided meditation, an interview, or a drama. Ward preaches about half the time. "Anybody might be asked to do a talk," she said. "It's not a clericalized process—on purpose" (Ward). And at the 5 p.m. Community in Seattle, the preaching is shared among the congregation each week. The presider begins, offering a brief reflection; then he or she opens up a conversation. The most compelling insights might come from anyone, lay or ordained.

And that's no accident. Shared preaching was part of the 5 p.m. Community's design. "Talking to clergy about launching new liturgies, I find they just don't follow a process," Skelton said. "They're like, 'Let's do this' or 'We think this group would want this.' It's just so simple-minded, it's scary." Instead, Skelton says, once an existing liturgy is at about 80 percent of capacity, the leader should begin a series of conversations to educate the congregation, listen for anxieties, and begin discussing hypothetical time slots. Then the leader should commission a discernment group to plan the worship experience, keeping the congregation updated regularly. "You have to be very careful that it comes out of the parish," Skelton said. "The rubber band wants to snap back organizationally, so having the parish feel tremendous ownership of it is key" (Skelton). Similarly, the Wilderness took planning seriously, too. Kate Eaton's work there led her to develop a four-step planning process she uses in consulting with congregations that are developing new expressions of worship (K. Eaton).

Following process helps congregations avoid the trap of creating ministries based on personal preference. Clergy, especially, bring their own sense of how worship, formation, and service to the community should look—and when those preferences morph into limitations, they can become boundaries to reaching people nearby. Broadening the development process can allow God to work in surprising, even uncomfortable, ways. "See where the Spirit is flowing, join it, and recognize that human barriers and designations of churchmanship and theology really don't matter," Williams said, reflecting on Tewkesbury Abbey's experience with Celebrate! "The leadership team must be mature enough to accept that God gives gifts in different ways for the building up of the body of Christ" (Williams, Personal interview 2).

Similarly—especially for Episcopal Church clergy formed by the liturgical movement of the twentieth century and the 1979 Book of Common Prayer—it helps to be open to worship other than Holy Eucharist. A new expression of worship is unlikely to be the "principal act of Christian worship on the Lord's Day" (BCP 13), so offering something other than Eucharist shouldn't offend prayer book strict constructionists. Of the congregations I visited, four were offering noneucharistic worship gatherings in their boundary-breaking ministries. Although the Wilderness in Denver always includes Holy Communion, Hartsuff recommends not being boxed in by that expectation. He notes that an unchurched person coming to Eucharist is immediately confronted with two of our thorniest theological questions: What happens to the bread and wine in consecration, and am I welcome to receive it? He points to the popularity of sung Compline at St. Mark's Cathedral in Seattle as an example of welcoming worship for people who are un- and de-churched ("Compline"). "It's accessible because it's 100 percent nonjudgmental," Hartsuff said. "It's shorter, it's noneucharistic, and it allows people to be in a completely receptive mode. You don't have to do anything but be there and receive" (Hartsuff).

Of course, new expressions of ministry may include no liturgy at all. Bundock in Manchester argues his church's school is a "four-hundred-year-old fresh expression," and he sees offering community space and a youth café as ways for the birds of the air to nest in the branches of St. James & Emmanuel (Bundock). In my congregation in Kansas City, we're also making space available for community use, both in our main building and through a renovation of our youth and community center across the street. In addition to meeting community needs through this resource, we're trying to build relationships with those who come our way and see how St. Andrew's might come alongside them and welcome them into the family. We've also created an incubator for social entrepreneurs developing market-based solutions to social issues, partnering with the social-entrepreneurship program at the University of Missouri-Kansas City ("About Us"). In our first significant mentoring relationship, St. Andrew's parishioners helped launch a new nonprofit, Empower the Parent to Empower the Child, which trains disadvantaged women for living-wage jobs as dog groomers, as well as teaching parenting and life skills ("About").

But if a new expression of ministry does come to fruition as a parallel congregation, like the Crossing, it's important that the inherited and new expressions of church take their relational energy and turn it toward each other. At best, that means more than worshiping together on major feasts; it means learning from each other and respecting the unique gifts for incarnating God's reign that each community bears. In Tewkesbury, members of Celebrate! come to the abbey for special events, like Christmas or baptisms, as well as children's programs and dances; but they also share stories of powerful ministry with abbey worshipers on several Sunday mornings a year. By the same token, abbey volunteers help put on Celebrate! worship each week and cook the hot meal in the school's kitchen. Similarly, in London, as new lay leaders rise up from the housing estate, they often worship with other Church@Five leaders at St. Barnabas. And at St. Barnabas, the Parish Church Council includes a seat for a Church@Five member. "It can be really good to have multiple congregations within the life of one church," Spellers said. "The key is they need to be mutually transformative" (Spellers). Perhaps it can be taken one step further, too: In the best of circumstances, multiple congregations would reflect the sacramental unity of marriage or the perichoretic dance of the Trinity itself—each partner demonstrating unique personhood within the unity of covenantal love.

What Matters Is the Meat

For those of us who struggle with perfectionism, the process of discerning new expressions of ministry offers many temptations to focus too much on form. Visiting and worshiping with these nine congregations, I could imagine (in the moment) my own church creating something similar to any or all of them. I try way too hard to do things right, and on some immature level, I hoped I'd come across "the thing" God wanted me to take back to St. Andrew's. I imagined returning from my sabbatical having been to the mountaintop. Instead, I climbed nine mountains and enjoyed the view from each of them. And still there remains the challenge of listening—to our Kansas City neighborhood, to Scripture and tradition, and to my congregation's heart.

Thankfully, for someone like me, the answer is that there is no right answer. The goal isn't to offer people a better version of Shady Inn, the steak house from my childhood. The goal is to offer them meat in whatever way best satisfies their hunger. Mobsby notes the same truth about the Moot Community's café in St. Mary Aldermary church in London. Sitting at a table maybe one hundred feet down the center aisle from the altar, sipping a latte, he explained, "We did a café because we wanted an excuse to build up hospitality and build up relationships with people who would never come and talk with us." But the point isn't the café. Nor is the point getting central London's hurting businesspeople to come to worship when their coffee cups are empty. The point is the Moot Community being a sacrament, an outward and visible conveyance of God's grace. "We expect God to do what God will do through what we're doing," Mobsby said. "Ultimately, that does get marked in Eucharist, as well as baptism, marriage, confirmation, and the rest. But the sacramental understanding is that the work of the Trinity in context starts from relationships." And the worship? For the most part, worship fosters "contemplative action" among the people who already are the *ecclesia*, the community of Christ's apostles. Sacramental worship "is much more about empowering the people of God, rather than encouraging unchurched people to go to church" (Mobsby).

I guess *that's* the right answer.

References

"About." Accessed January 20, 2016. *http://www.epeckc.org/?page_id=11.*

"About Us." Accessed January 20, 2016. *http://reddoorcenter.com/about-us.*

Archbishop's Council on Mission and Public Affairs. *Mission-Shaped Church: Church Planting and Fresh Expressions in a Changing Context.* New York: Seabury Books, 2010.

Bundock, Nick. Personal interview by John Spicer. October 24, 2014.

"Compline." Accessed January 20, 2016. *http://www.saintmarks.org/experience/worship/season-of-lent.*

Dickinson, Beth. Personal interview by John Spicer. October 26, 2014.

Eaton, Kate. "Services." Accessed August 31, 2015. *http://www.mishkhah.com/about/services.*

Eaton, Peter. Personal interview by John Spicer. September 20, 2014.

Edson, Ben. Personal interview by John Spicer. May 1, 2014.

Everett, Isaac. Personal interview 1 by John Spicer. May 8, 2014.

"FAQ." Accessed September 12, 2015. *http://www.portlandabbey.org/about/faq.*

"The Five Rhythms of Grace." Accessed November 16, 2015. *http://www.stjamesandemmanuel.org/the-five-rhythms-of-grace.*

Hartsuff, Jadon. Personal interview 1 by John Spicer. June 12, 2014.

Kurdzeil, Annie. Personal interview by John Spicer. September 8, 2014.

Mills-Curran, Mary Beth. Personal interview by John Spicer. September 4, 2014.

Mobsby, Ian. Personal interview by John Spicer. October 20, 2014.

Mullen, Melanie. Personal interview 2 by John Spicer. November 3, 2014.

Ruffle, Wendy. Personal interview 3 by John Spicer. October 12, 2014.

Skelton, Melissa. Personal interview by John Spicer. September 10, 2014.

Spellers, Stephanie. Personal interview by John Spicer. September 10, 2014.

"Spirituality." Accessed January 14, 2016. *http://www.portlandabbey.org/about/spirituality.*

Ward, Karen. Personal interview 2 by John Spicer. September 30, 2014.

Williams, Paul. Personal interview 1 by John Spicer. July 17, 2014.

———. Personal interview 2 by John Spicer. October 10, 2014.

6

How Will You Empower Strong Leadership and Plan for Governance?

"In the beginning when God created the heavens and the earth, the earth was a formless void and darkness covered the face of the deep, while a wind from God swept over the face of the waters. Then God said, 'Let there be light'; and there was light. And God saw that the light was good."
—Genesis 1:1–4

GOING BACK TO THE STORY of my favorite childhood steak house, Shady Inn: It closed in 2001, ending a fifty-four-year run. My hunch is that the owners took the proceeds from the sale and enjoyed a well-deserved rest. But what if they had felt a calling to satisfy hungry people in new ways? After fifty-four years of offering six cuts of steak, would they have had the capacity to make a change?

And what about my parish? Like most congregations, it's seen huge changes, especially in the past fifty years or so. In 1964, one year before I was born, St. Andrew's went through its greatest change to that point, bidding farewell to the Rev. Dr. Earle Jewell. Dr. Jewell had been rector since 1938, leading St. Andrew's through the Great Depression, financial shortfall, and the Second

World War; through the fight over racial segregation in a deeply segregated city; through the assassination of a president, the beginning of real conflict in Vietnam, and social changes Dr. Jewell probably barely fathomed. He led St. Andrew's to become the third largest congregation in The Episcopal Church, according to Dr. Jewell himself (Jewell 4), and he sounded the missional call to plant a new parish in then-growing south Kansas City (complete with a worship space that looks just like St. Andrew's, only shrunken). His time as rector ended in 1964, two years before the peak of Episcopal Church membership in 1966.

In the time since Dr. Jewell retired, St. Andrew's has navigated choppy waters, along with the rest of The Episcopal Church. It's seen school desegregation, the civil rights movement, and Black Lives Matter; AIDS, the gay rights movement, and same-sex marriage; a new prayer book, "permissive rubrics," and women's ordination. St. Andrew's itself has now been blessed by the ministry of female clergy, black clergy, and gay clergy. And, after Dr. Jewell's twenty-six-year reign, we've transitioned among nine rectors in the following fifty-two years.

Now his painted portrait hangs in the Jewell Room, St. Andrew's antique-filled reception space. His steady gaze follows you around the room as you sip coffee and welcome newcomers on Sunday morning. I feel it following me especially. Dr. Jewell doesn't smile. He looks down with the intensity of one who's set the bar.

Today, as everyone knows, the institutional church is facing new challenges, as many of the forces that supported its growth in Dr. Jewell's day fade away or reverse. Since 1964, we've moved from social expectations driving church attendance (and the "right" parish opening doors to good social and business contacts) to church as one option among many on a busy Sunday. If you want to network, hanging out at the coffeehouse will probably take you farther than coming to coffee hour.

The church and its leaders (myself included) aren't exactly known to be gifted with flexible adaptation to new realities. Just as I actually like Rite I and Rite II on Sunday mornings, I like knowing the tasks I'm supposed to do—offer meaningful liturgies, preach a good sermon, teach a compelling class, end a vestry meeting as quickly as possible. And I like it when the results of those efforts reflect their quality. If you preach good sermons and teach good classes, you should see more folks in the pews and more pledges on file, as time goes on. That's how it worked for Dr. Jewell—and by all accounts, he was, indeed, an outstanding preacher and teacher.

But Dr. Jewell also shared some wiring with today's new ministry entrepreneurs: He understood the importance of deep investment in people. His book—perfectly titled, *You Can If You Want To!*, complete with the exclamation point of clerical self-assurance—proudly proclaims that he had more than thirty thousand pastoral counseling appointments across his forty-one years of active ministry (Jewell 4). That's 732 people a year, or three people a day, five days a week. It makes me wonder where he found time to run the congregation, which institutional memory affirms he most certainly did. But it also reinforces the reports I hear from older parishioners even today. One man loves to tell me how Dr. Jewell met with him and "sicked two guys" on him (pastorally) as soon as he and his wife came to the church. Like today's church-based community organizers, Dr. Jewell knew about apostles' call to build webs of relationships. The difference was that, back then, the people looking for relationships walked into the web.

Some still do, but now we have to go to them more intentionally than we used to. And when we do, the Holy Spirit breathes new expressions of ministry into being—though they, like creation itself, tend to start out as formless voids. As those new ministries arise, like sparks fanned in dried grass to light new fire for an Easter Vigil, our task and our challenge is to care for them. We are called to "midwife the work of the Spirit," writes the Rev. Tom Brackett, missioner for new church starts and missional initiatives for The Episcopal Church (Brackett 36).

We do that work through leadership and governance. But both ordained leaders' training and the churches they've inherited are largely wired for a different time. Brackett argues the theological frameworks of most denominations, including The Episcopal Church, "were cobbled together at a time when the Church's authority was granted by the state and the Church operated from the center of society. In those halcyon days," Brackett writes, church leaders' calling was "to bring God to the world—to introduce the Christian life to the 'lost' out there. The world changed, but the calling has yet to be recast" (Brackett 37–38).

There is no shortage of church-leadership gurus, and I'm certainly not one of them. But I've been blessed to visit with people who are midwifing church without knowing precisely how it will mature, people who are managing the work of fitting delicate new creations of ministry into the sometimes unforgiving structures of polity, bylaws, and congregational leadership culture. They've had to ask, "How will we empower strong leadership and plan for governance?" I have not, unfortunately, been able to speak with Dr. Jewell about all this. But I know he's watching, along with the rest of the great company of saints, to see how we steward the Spirit's work today. Maybe someday, his portrait will smile.

Leading without a Map

Of the congregations I visited, the Cathedral of St. Paul in Boston and the Crossing have evolved the most well-defined governance relationship between "mother church" and new expression. But in the beginning, they were negotiating the steps of the collaborative dance as all new expressions do. The Very Rev. John (Jep) Streit, cathedral dean, imagined the new effort would be a Sunday night service for college students and other young adults; but the cathedral's new associate, the Rev. Stephanie Spellers, had a different idea from the start—developing a community that would become a fresh expression of church. One of the most crucial steps in the Crossing's journey was Streit's initial willingness to take a risk with Spellers's vision. "There had to be a senior clergyperson who was willing to say, 'I can't quite picture what you're talking about, but go for it,'" Spellers explained (Spellers). Remembered Streit: "Stephanie said early on, 'I need this to be my own thing; I don't want you hovering too closely.' So we respected that and let it take its own direction" (Streit).

Part of the Crossing's developing autonomy was about money. When Spellers began, an outside fellowship paid her salary, so the cathedral didn't own the position financially. After three years, when the fellowship ended, Spellers began raising funds to augment support from the cathedral and the diocese. But at that point, she wasn't on the cathedral staff, instead working as a speaker and consultant on radical welcome while maintaining clergy leadership of the Crossing. "It was a little gray; I wasn't her boss," Streit said (Streit). So for a couple of years, the Crossing functioned separately from the cathedral. Because of its own fundraising, the Crossing "expected a level of autonomy that few other cathedral congregations actually get," said Isaac Everett, minister for liturgical arts. After Spellers left, the relationship with the cathedral took center stage when the Crossing experienced its first budget deficit—for which the cathedral was responsible because it officially held the Crossing's finances. The experience led the Crossing and cathedral to work more collaboratively. "Prior to that, there was an emotional drive for the Crossing to feel a degree of its own autonomy; that shifted a little bit," Everett said (Everett).

Internally, the Crossing managed its ministry through "leadership circles" for worship, community life, and social action. Eventually, the community-life circle morphed into an elected Council—nearly a miniversty. The Council creates and oversees an annual budget, in collaboration with the cathedral finance committee; oversees fundraising; oversees the work of other Crossing groups and committees; makes hiring and firing recommendations to the cathedral dean and chapter (leadership body); and maintains relationships with the cathedral and diocese, including naming a Crossing representative for the cathedral chapter (The Crossing). The Council, and its relationship with the cathedral, is still a work in progress. The Council "is a little bit like a jellyfish," Streit said. "It's new and figuring itself out" (Streit). The primary point of interaction is money, and it's a relationship of grace. The cathedral continues to subsidize some of the Crossing's operation, and the Crossing stays in close touch with the cathedral finance committee through the year.

Though a very different new expression of ministry, the Wilderness in Denver was also designed as a decentralized, collaborative effort from the beginning. Kate Eaton, spouse of the dean, led the work to create and sustain the liturgy, but she also took pains to ensure that responsibility for ongoing planning and execution rested in groups of laypeople. As it evolved into Kate Eaton's Mishkhah model of worship design, separate teams take responsibility for liturgy writing, visual arts, music, hospitality, and communications ("Mishkhah: Enter Into Mystery"). The conveners of those groups assemble regularly for "discovery nights," when they plan worship for an upcoming eight-week "season," Eaton said (K. Eaton). The decision to share presiding among staff clergy also helped keep the focus on worship of God rather than the personality of a clergy leader, explained the Rt. Rev. Peter Eaton, former dean (P. Eaton). But Kate Eaton's leadership was central to the service's spiritual and aesthetic power to draw people from beyond the cathedral's membership. "It *did* become a personality cult around Kate, and I'm not sure that's all bad," said the Rev. Jadon Hartsuff, who now oversees the Wilderness. Her leadership and continuity of presence garnered the large number of volunteers necessary to put on a liturgy as elaborate as the Wilderness (Hartsuff).

At St. Andrew and All Souls (SAAS) in Portland, the presence of a strong, visionary leader has made all the difference in bringing together the faithful remnant of a 121-year-old congregation and a handful of young spiritual seekers. The fact that this new creation of church hasn't failed is remarkable, given the dynamics associated with change, loss of power, and loss of control. Lines could well have hardened after the first year of the Rev. Karen Ward's time there when the bishop extended the terms of the incumbent wardens, limiting Ward's power to push past the governance status quo. At times, when members of the faithful remnant have felt threatened by specific changes Ward wanted, conflict has surfaced—for example: "Tree-gate." A neighborhood group (and potential community partner for the congregation) wanted to plant trees on SAAS' property. Where Ward saw an opportunity to build a relationship with young, environmentally conscious neighborhood residents ("Portland is one of the tree-hugging capitals of the world for young adults," Ward said; "the Sierra Club is like a church to them"), longtime members saw the burden of tending the new plantings and the risk that roots would harm the sidewalk and water main. The conflict went all the way to the leadership body. Ward argued the neighborhood group, or newer members of the congregation, would have been happy to take responsibility for pruning and watering (not to mention the watering from God that Portland is known for). "But they were just thinking of the past," Ward said—a time before the congregation saw itself in close partnership with the community and when an aging and shrinking cadre of parishioners found themselves responsible for everything. "I backed off; I didn't want to get into this Tree-gate. So I tabled it—for now." But despite the conflict inherent in the blended church family, the newcomers and the old guard have learned to live together. Ward notes that "the only people who have left the church have done so through funerals" (Ward).

Much of that stability-in-conflict comes from the strength of Ward's leadership. Neither contingent has had to wonder what lies ahead because Ward is a case study in "plan your work and work your plan." Following the model she used at Church of the Apostles in Seattle, Ward is leading the congregation in forming a rule of life specific to SAAS, including virtues (e.g., welcome, feeding, hospitality) and spiritual practices (e.g., daily prayer, worship attendance, giving). Specifying these virtues and practices gives the congregation's leadership a yardstick by which to measure its work. "We will refer to the rule in everything we do," Ward said. "When I give my reports to the Bishop's Advisory Committee, I'll say, 'Let's look at one of the principles of our rule of life; how are we doing with that this month?'—and we'll reflect on that." Though Ward has congregation members read classic rules from St. Benedict and St. Francis, and though she leads very directly in crafting a rule for the congregation, the result is specific to the people of SAAS and the people they're called to serve. And— noteworthy for a denomination sometimes perceived to suffer from a lack of theological specificity—the rule will articulate directly what "progressive Catholic Christianity" means at SAAS. "My friends have a bullshit meter," Ward said. "You have to be honest, have integrity, and have conviction. This can't be 'anything goes'; you have to stand for something and know what it is and why. I know exactly what we believe in" (Ward).

Strong leadership also marked the experience of St. Paul's in Seattle, but there the model was more collaborative. The Rt. Rev. Melissa Skelton, who was the rector at the time, knew from growing attendance that the moment had come to add another service. She held a series of parish meetings to teach about congregational growth and how near-capacity services can limit it. Listening to comments from the meetings, she gauged the congregation's readiness to launch a new service without getting into its potential style or time slot (though she wanted an evening offering). Eventually she heard support for an evening service—"an expansion of the parish's Anglo-Catholic identity that we would commission a highly trusted team to work on," Skelton explained (Skelton). From discernment, through development of the liturgy, and through the 5 p.m. Community's first year, Skelton was intentional about crafting and supporting the experience, ensuring it shared the same status as the parish's other worship offerings. "As rector, Melissa convened the original talking groups and planning groups that created this; she was at 5 o'clock presiding almost every Sunday," said Mark Taylor, a member of that liturgy's design team and former senior warden. "That signaled this was not an orphan; it was part of the core life of the parish" (Taylor).

Skelton's collaborative wiring also led her to raise up laypeople as "community developers" for each of St. Paul's services, including the new 5 p.m. Community. Originally, that role was "to be a mini-me," Skelton said. The community developers trained lay ministers in various roles and ensured assigned people showed up to serve each Sunday. They also presided at the coffee hour following their services—coordinating refreshments, making announcements, and connecting newcomers with other parishioners. The community developers were responsible for newcomer follow-up, too. Skelton's intent was to delegate responsibility for the Sunday morning experience to "someone who, with the rector, owns its quality, its failure or success," Skelton said. "It's at the liturgical service level that somebody will stay or leave, feel affiliated or not. What's important isn't the visitor's attitude toward the general parish; it's about what happens to me in this liturgy and at coffee hour, first and foremost" (Skelton). And it worked—both in terms of building a high-quality experience for newcomers and in terms of practicing collaborative leadership. "Melissa was really good at empowering people to be entrepreneurs, to take initiative," Taylor noted. "She was masterful at keeping in connection to these entrepreneurial centers as rector, so that she knew what was going on and what the leader was up to. The community developers knew they reported to her, and she knew what was going on—but she didn't have to do it" (Taylor).

Leadership is also key for Celebrate!, the expression of Tewkesbury Abbey in its neighboring social-housing "estate." The pioneer minister for Celebrate!, the Rev. Wendy Ruffle, strikes an amazing balance as she practices deeply personal, pastoral investment in individuals while building their capacity and opportunity to lead. Part of her success is her awareness of herself and the needs of her church community. For now, Celebrate! "is about my personality; it's very one-to-one ministry," she explained. "But I've worked very hard from day 1 to make this about the community. Because of the brokenness here [in the housing estate], it's very vulnerable as a church." One way she makes the ministry about the community is by narrating the leadership process, using meetings as formational moments with people whose social experience has made them question both their capacity to lead and the willingness of the dominant culture to welcome it. Ruffle described the journey of a new Christian there who has grown in her confidence to the point of leading prayers during Celebrate! worship. "To take responsibility for something as big as that is quite a step," Ruffle said. "This is growing them as leaders— walking alongside them, releasing people in their giftings, recognizing where they are, seeing what God's doing in all of that, and then encouraging it" (Ruffle).

Since Celebrate! began in late 2010 as something of a one-woman show, Ruffle slowly has been able to let go of facets of ministry. Celebrate! planning group members now choose themes for weekly worship based on the Scriptures of the day, prepare and lead prayers, and plan crafts and games. "These are beautiful moments, actually," Ruffle said. "You just think, 'These guys own this now.' It's like this beautiful white dove has had its wings

pinned in; you hold that dove in your hand and then just let it fly."
At a practical level, Ruffle recognizes her work to empower people
and build their leadership capacity will be what makes or breaks
Celebrate! for the long term. "We need to make the community
stable so that eventually, when God calls me away, someone else
can step straight in" (Ruffle).

Developing the God-given capacity of marginalized people is
also how the Rev. Helen Shannon sees her call with Church@Five
in London. Like Ruffle, Shannon works hard to evoke and affirm
the leadership gifts—and inherent belovedness—of housing-estate
residents. For Shannon, formation for leadership is a proclamation
of the reign of God in a success-oriented culture marked by class
division. "Society says the people here are worth nothing, that they
can do nothing," Shannon explains. "Many of them are jobless;
many families have been jobless for generations. But the kingdom
of God comes in and says, 'No, you are worth so much; God has
called you to do so much.' We just want to help them achieve all
that God's got for them" (Shannon, Personal interview 1).

The pastoral intensity of Church@Five takes a team of ministers. About ten St. Barnabas people have chosen to move there,
and other members serve there in shorter-term capacities. "I don't
have the sole relation," Shannon said. "I don't need to know everything; I trust my team." Having a variety of people involved from
St. Barnabas builds connectivity between the "mother church" and
the new expression, which Shannon says is just as important for
the formation of St. Barnabas as it is for Church@Five. "It changes
St. Barnabas, because then St. Barnabas knows the poor," she
explained. "They're not just reading about them; they know them"
(Shannon, Personal interview 2).

Conflict, collaboration, pastoral relationships, lay empowerment—all these can be leadership challenges in new expressions
of church. But so can a blank slate. In Richmond, St. Paul's knew
it needed more capacity in its downtown mission and called a new
priest to lead it. That priest was to be both a part of congregational life and a bridge to take that life outside the church, "leading us out into the community in experimental ways, looking for
fresh opportunities to connect with people," said the Rev. Wallace

Adams-Riley, rector (Adams-Riley). For that new downtown missioner, the Rev. Melanie Mullen, the role was very open-ended.
"There was a sense of, 'We want you to be free to figure it out
for us and tell us what it should be,'" she said. That gave her the
opportunity to hear the community's needs, try new things, and
risk failure safely. But it also presented a challenge in identifying
what "downtown mission" really was and then sharing it broadly.
"My first ordained mistake was not figuring out how to communi-
cate what we were doing to the entire parish," Mullen said. "People just thought, 'If Melanie's involved, it must be about those guys
with the beards'" (Mullen).

In St. Mary's County, Maryland, leaders also hit a stumbling
block in specifying what they sought to accomplish. But there, the
issue was specifying too much too soon—and thereby strengthen-
ing resistance to change. The parishes of Ascension, Trinity, and St.
George's created two new expressions of shared ministry—Gather
Eat Pray and Thirsty Theology. At the same time, the clergy and
lay leaders looked at how they did the church's business and realized that duplicating work at each congregation was stewarding
resources poorly and limiting their missional capacity. So they
proposed creating a new level of governance to foster collaborative ministry and reduce operating costs. The proposed entity was
called a Multi-Parish Council (MPC), made up of clergy and lay
leaders from the three participating parishes. As originally con-
ceived, the body would have overseen shared ministries and driven
the congregations toward sharing expenses, including staff and
(eventually) clergy. The MPC would have held and administered
the money parishes budgeted for personnel. It also would have had
power to review parish budgets and recommend ways the congregations could share personnel costs and administrative expenses.
And it could have assessed fines on congregations that chose not
to implement its resource-sharing proposals. The intent was to
build a culture not just of collaborative ministry but collaborative decision-making on issues involving "not a couple of hundred
dollars here and there, but real money," explained the Rev. Greg
Syler, rector at St. George's. With practice in sharing resources and
"big decision-making," the stage would be set when staff or clergy

transitions came, enabling the congregations to consider sharing staff or clergy while remaining autonomous parishes (Syler, Personal interview 2).

The prospect of sanctions on parishes from an outside entity was clearly an overreach. "The language of penalties caused a lot of reactivity," Syler said. "After the Baby Boom, The Episcopal Church bought into the one-priest–one-parish mentality. I've had a hard time trying to prove to local congregations that I'm not in this for a corporate takeover" (Syler, Personal interview 2). Now, with the untimely death of Ascension's rector and Trinity's decision not to take part in the Multi-Parish Council, Ascension and St. George's have carried on with their discernment about how to rethink the institution in the interests of stewardship and missional energy. At this writing, the congregations have agreed to yoke—sharing ministries (such as Thirsty Theology), sharing a vestry or creating an additional layer of leadership, and sharing clergy; but maintaining separate finances and property, and offering worship at both locations. Right now, this degree of institutional rethinking is as much risk as the congregations can handle—at least letting the horse out of the barn, even if the horse is only slowly plodding down the path (Syler, E-mail correspondence 3).

Lessons from the Field: Leadership

Among clergy, at least, parish search processes are infamous for seeking candidates who don't exist. Congregations seem to be looking for a wise and seasoned leader who has served a long career in multiple parishes but who also somehow has a bubbly spouse, small children, and the boundless energy of youth. At the risk of committing a similar sin and painting portraits of people or churches that don't exist (with the exception of Dr. Jewell, of course), here are several characteristics of leadership common across the new ministries I visited.

First, the congregation's rector (senior pastor) must be willing to empower and support a leader for the new ministry. That may not be as easy as it sounds because several stumbling blocks can get in the way of everyone's best intentions. The rector and ministry leader need to share a vision of what they're seeking to build. The ministry leader needs to know what's expected with as much specificity as the local context will allow—what are the "deliverables," and what is the rector willing to leave to the interplay of the ministry leader's gifts and the power of the Holy Spirit? The ministry leader needs clear areas of oversight based on the boundaries God is asking the congregation to beat (e.g., focusing on a demographic, a geographic location, a cultural group). The rector needs to walk the fine line of engaged supervision, staying in close touch with the ministry and its leader without micromanaging. In that relationship, the ministry leader needs the rector's supportive attention, advocacy, and perhaps even protection as the ministry leader inevitably disappoints constituencies in the congregation (and perhaps him-/herself). Maybe most of all, the ministry leader needs time. Deeply relational ministry demands slow, one-on-one investment in one child of God after another.

Second, the new ministry leader must be willing and able to lead. There is no substitute for the abilities and passions that God has wired into several of the individuals I met in my congregational visits, giftedness their colleagues readily acknowledge. "Personal leadership is the most vital characteristic of them all," said the Rev. Paul Williams in Tewkesbury. "I am absolutely convinced we would not be in the position we are without Wendy [Ruffle], who is totally dedicated to relational evangelism, to the area, to the people" (Williams). Similarly, the Rev. Henry Kendal in London says, "Helen [Shannon] is a force of nature, and actually you need that in a missioner" (Kendal). That missional force reveals itself in a variety of ways, including immersing oneself in the congregation's context, being willing to experiment and risk, engaging areas of difference (and potential conflict), building relationships naturally, and leading people away from fear. Sometimes the strength of an individual leader can bump up against structures or personalities (a bishop might wince at Ward's advice to plant churches first and ask permission later). But as a host of angels, and Jesus himself, advises in Scripture, "Fear not!"

Third, resist the temptation to identify a boundary-crossing effort with an individual leader. Instead, the more gifted the leader is, the harder he or she must push both to raise up others and to delegate responsibility to them. In Tewkesbury, for example, former abbey volunteer and ordinand-in-training Lara Bloom said succession at Celebrate! is "a massive question mark" because of the deeply relational ministry involved and how it is identified with Ruffle herself (Bloom). Being aware of the risk, leaders can work to build up other leaders and delegate to them—and, as Ruffle does, they can narrate the identity they seek: "This is God's church, not my church," she said. "It's the community's church, something we do together" (Ruffle).

Fourth, leaders need to connect new ministries intentionally with the existing church. Skelton, formerly in Seattle, not only engaged the congregation in discerning the shape of the new 5 p.m. Community and invested herself in it deeply to affirm its place in St. Paul's worship life; she also invited parishioners to experience the new ministry. "We did a pretty good job of trying to prepare the parish for what was new, and what wasn't new, about the service; and pretty much everybody cycled in and out of it at some point," Taylor said. Several Sunday morning worshipers came to be part of a 5 p.m. choir, which also signaled the new experience wasn't new as much as "more St. Paul's," Taylor said (Taylor).

Finally, and perhaps most importantly, new ministries thrive in a collaborative leadership culture. Fresh expressions writer Ian Mobsby argues the leader in this kind of system not only sets aside the trappings of clerical authority but actually follows Jesus's model of kenosis, or self-emptying, in actively giving power away. "You need indigenous leadership, and that means you move from the idea of the priest as the cure of souls, with a lot of people helping him out, to something that looks more like the priest as the first amongst equals," Mobsby said. "You've got to let go of being in control" and move toward an accountability model he calls "shared episcope" (oversight) instead (Mobsby, Personal interview). Of the congregations I visited, St. Paul's Cathedral in Boston and the Crossing manifested this most clearly. The Crossing's culture has been built on lay empowerment and shared leadership from the beginning, and the cathedral leadership is willing to engage the Crossing's Council in a dance of oversight rather than control. But nearly all the new ministries I encountered have some kind of collaborative leadership group among clergy and laypeople or involve laypeople in liturgical roles typically taken by clergy.

In my setting, as St. Andrew's seeks to beat our boundaries and open ourselves up to our Kansas City neighborhood, that collaborative leadership culture is probably our greatest asset—but it hasn't come about with the flip of a switch. In our parish, not only do we carry the history of Dr. Jewell's benevolent dictatorship, we also have a (probably unintentional) icon of clergy-centric leadership right above the high altar. In the stained-glass tryptic of Andrew, Peter, and our Lord, the central panel presents Jesus clothed in a cope, alb, and cincture—the ultimate rector. We've taken steps away from that implicit model in the past few years, aided by a senior warden, Stephen Rock, whose day job is being an organizational change-management consultant and writer.[1] We've reorganized the executive team's responsibilities so that the clergy and wardens each oversee a collection of ministries, and vestry members bear responsibility (either in a liaison or a convening role) for commissions that carry out the parish's temporal and spiritual life. Our financial policies and procedures require vestry liaisons to approve staff expenditures over a certain amount, to invest these leaders in both their canonically required oversight of temporal affairs and in their growing exercise of collaborative ministry leadership. It's definitely a work in progress, and some lay leaders are more willing to live into the role than others. But I think the same Lord who breathed out the Holy Spirit on his friends to send them into the world as his ambassadors (John 20:21–22) wants us to push the boundaries of our clericalism and benefit from the leadership gifts of all.

Lessons from the Field: Governance

As Greg Syler said in some frustration about his experience with the MPC in St. Mary's County, Maryland, "The institutional

---

1. Stephen Rock, *Manager's Guide to Navigating Change* (New York: McGraw-Hill, 2013).

church will not only feel threatened by new ministries, it will try to extinguish new ministries as quickly as they emerge" (Syler, Personal interview 2). The institution's DNA includes self-preservation, and its equilibrium is the status quo—so those charged with stewarding new ministries need to ensure the organization doesn't live fully into its wiring.

A relatively simple, but potentially transformative, way to support new ministries is simply to give them a place at the table. If a new expression functions like a congregation, it should have official representation on the parish leadership body. Giving a new ministry voice and vote says, in an outward and visible way, that this new effort to beat boundaries and embody church is just as real, just as proper, as the Sunday morning Rite I and Rite II communities. Without the official imprimatur of a bylaws change, the institutional culture will likely push back toward the status quo. Mobsby says there's formational value in this process, too, helping the congregation confront differentials of power. "You almost need to unsettle the traditional thing to show that these new ministries are equals, and not the church's grandchildren whom you can tell what to do," Mobsby said. "You've got to be prepared to let go of power, do things you feel uncomfortable about, and listen to people you don't agree with" (Mobsby, Personal interview). Of the congregations I visited, new ministries have representatives on the leadership body in Boston, Denver, Seattle, and London.

Similarly, consider giving new ministries some autonomy once they have their ecclesial legs under them. As with the Crossing, autonomy empowers new ministries to live increasingly into the measure of the full stature of the body of Christ (Eph. 4:13). It helps build a sense of corporate responsibility among the participants in areas like generosity, stewardship, administration, and conflict resolution—marks of maturing communities. In addition, sharing responsibility and power like this helps form the larger church culture in a boundary-beating direction, toward embrace of difference. Mobsby argues it makes the parish church more expressive of the nature of God, representing the Trinitarian mystery of unity in diversity rather than adopting a model of unity through control. "As the Trinity models unity in diversity, where all three persons are co-equal, so should the Church reflect the sense of being a body of co-equal persons in one community" (Mobsby, *God Unknown: The Trinity in Contemporary Spirituality and Mission* 74).

Of course, as the story from St. Mary's County, Maryland, reveals, timing is everything. In 2013 and 2014, as the three parishes began exploring creative possibilities for sharing ministry and resources while retaining their individual identities, it seemed to be a kairotic time, the rich moment when human experience intersects with divine purpose and reveals God's reign "on earth, as it is in heaven." Unfortunately, the desire for change encouraged parish leaders to go too far too fast and got in the way of a holy moment; and the MPC was basically shelved. That is, it was shelved until the death of the Rev. Sherrill Page, rector of Ascension. That was precisely the sort of moment for which the MPC had been intended to prepare the way. But God's timing trumps our stumbling steps, and now Ascension and St. George's are working together to create a yoking relationship similar to what the MPC imagined. Still, the cautionary tale is good for the rest of us to heed: Don't try to change governance too much or too quickly, and be especially attentive to whose ox your change will gore.

Midwifing Fire

If your church is of a certain age, you probably have a Dr. Jewell, too. Maybe he looks down on you and your vestry meetings as he does on mine. Rather than holding us up to his standard, bronzed and polished with time and the convenient amnesia that follows golden ages, I think even Dr. Jewell himself might be more interested in the sparks of new ministry that extend church relationship past our boundaries and into people's lived experience. So as I feel his eyes following me, I will remember to take myself mentally out of the Jewell Room, through the narthex, and out the door. Because there, on Holy Saturday, a member of our Scout troop lights the new fire, the spark that lights the flame atop the paschal candle. I was struck, last Easter, watching a thirteen-year-old in his dress uniform perform what, for me, could only have been magic—or the movement of the Holy Spirit. He struck his flint into a loose handful of dry grass, and we saw the smoke waft upward. Then he picked up that grass nest, cradled it before his lips, blew gently—and fire was birthed in his hands. That moment, that image, is the portrait of new ministry, an icon of midwifing the Holy Spirit's work.

References

Adams-Riley, Wallace. Personal interview by John Spicer. November 5, 2014.

Bloom, Lara. Personal interview by John Spicer. October 14, 2014.

Brackett, Thomas. "Midwifing the Movement of the Spirit." In *Ancient Faith, Future Mission: Fresh Expressions in the Sacramental Tradition,* edited by Steven Croft, Ian Mobsby, and Stephanie Spellers, 34–49. New York: Church Publishing, 2010.

The Crossing. *Leadership Structure Task Force Report.* Boston: The Crossing, 2013.

Eaton, Kate. Personal interview 2 by John Spicer. September 20, 2014.

Eaton, Peter. Personal interview by John Spicer. September 20, 2014.

Everett, Isaac. Personal interview 1 by John Spicer. May 8, 2014.

Hartsuff, Jadon. Personal interview 2 by John Spicer. September 21, 2014.

Jewell, Earle B. *You Can if You Want To!* Kansas City, MO: Midwest Publishing, 1968.

Kendal, Henry. Personal interview 2 by John Spicer. October 16, 2014.

"Mishkhah: Enter Into Mystery." Accessed January 20, 2016. *http://www.mishkhah.com.*

Mobsby, Ian. *God Unknown: The Trinity in Contemporary Spirituality and Mission.* Norwich, UK: Canterbury Press, 2012.

———. Personal interview by John Spicer. October 20, 2014.

Mullen, Melanie. Personal interview 2 by John Spicer. November 3, 2014.

Ruffle, Wendy. Personal interview 2 by John Spicer. October 10, 2014.

Shannon, Helen. Personal interview 1 by John Spicer. July 8, 2014.

———. Personal interview 2 by John Spicer. October 16, 2014.

Skelton, Melissa. Personal interview by John Spicer. September 10, 2014.

Spellers, Stephanie. Personal interview by John Spicer. September 10, 2014.

Streit, John P. Personal interview 1 by John Spicer. July 24, 2014.

Syler, Greg. E-mail correspondence 3 with John Spicer. December 17, 2015.

———. Personal interview 2 by John Spicer. November 7, 2014.

Taylor, Mark. Personal interview by John Spicer. October 3, 2014.

Ward, Karen. Personal interview 2 by John Spicer. September 30, 2014.

Williams, Paul. Personal interview 2 by John Spicer. October 10, 2014.

7

How Will You Identify Success and Failure?

"The kingdom of heaven is like a merchant in search of fine pearls; on finding one pearl of great value, he went and sold all that he had and bought it." —Matthew 13:45-46

YESTERDAY, MY PARISH HAD ITS ANNUAL meeting (only our 102nd, as opposed to the 378th for St. George's in Valley Lee, Maryland). Overall, things are going pretty well, but it's interesting to hear how people describe it, myself included. One dear older woman has told me more than once that when she gets up on Sunday morning, she can't wait to get to church because "the Spirit is so active; there's just so much joy. I want to skip when I come through those doors!" Praise God for that. Then we have the people, like the master in Jesus's parable, who want a careful accounting of what the church has done with the talents with which it's been entrusted. "We added a third clergy position in 2013, a pastor for young adults and families," asks another parishioner. "What return has that investment shown? Why don't we see more people in the pews?" It is right, and a good (if not joyful) thing, to hear questions like that.

So, when I reported to the congregation on annual meeting Sunday, I tried to reflect both kinds of success because both kinds matter. We've seen increases in membership, participation in children's and adult formation, pledging units, and pledged income.

Praise God for all of that—but it's not the full measure of success. For example: Homeless and working-poor people found not just lunch at a downtown feeding program but someone to talk and pray with them, too. Kids at a local elementary school learned how to grow vegetables in a food desert—and wanted to eat them. People who don't give a dime to the church were loved and cared for through times of grief. Three hundred kids were taught and fed at a school in rural Haiti. A social entrepreneur found contacts, support, advice, money, and board members in our parish, enough to launch her ministry to train single parents for living-wage jobs. People donned Mardi Gras beads, ate buckets of shrimp, and laughed the night away.

Some of those examples of success will show up on the parochial report, and some won't. And alongside the successes are plenty of failures, too—mostly sins of omission, but times we missed the mark nonetheless.

The life of religious institutions can sometimes feel inherently adversarial. I am marked (maybe scarred) by the first stops in my professional life. I had trained to be a journalist and worked at a newspaper briefly before becoming speechwriter and deputy press secretary for the governor of Missouri. Every day, I saw the back and forth between those in a position of public trust and those who inherently distrusted the government. The reporters wanted to play "gotcha" with the press secretary and, if possible, the governor, while our job was to deflect criticism and project an aura of success. I stayed in the position a grand total of eighteen months. My boss, the press secretary, kept a constant supply of Mylanta in his desk drawer and made a career change a couple of months after I moved on. It wasn't a healthy environment. Perhaps I apply this model to congregational life more than I should, but it can feel similar. The need for institutional success, coupled with a hermeneutic of suspicion among church members, can lead to a culture of distrust in church. And, of course, that distrust expresses itself especially when congregations face hard times. "It's easy to be generous when you're on a roll," as Paul Simon sings; "It's hard to be grateful when you're out of control" (Simon). Our recent annual meeting felt pretty good. But, unless you're Dr. Jewell, you can't expect it will always go that way.

And if we're faithful about beating our boundaries, we can be assured it won't. Going to the edge of our comfort zones and building relationships with people in new ways—that's risky, entrepreneurial work; by definition, we will fail sometimes. That doesn't tend to sit well with American congregations because our culture's high doctrine of secular success is a big part of the contextual soup in which our churches swim. If we start something, we want to see it grow, and we want to see evidence of growth fairly quickly. Reflecting that adversarial congregational dynamic, ordained leaders can find ourselves feeling like press secretaries, trying to justify not just our work in the moment but our calling as clergy. And that defensiveness can make us go too far in rejecting "worldly" measures of success, arguing that it's changed hearts, not numbers, that matter.

In this exciting, risky, apostolic time, congregations that buy into that reporter/press secretary model are doomed. First, the theology is awful: If we are one body with many members, the hands and the feet can't live in mutual suspicion (1 Cor. 12:12–31). And practically, do we really want the government's results?

Instead, those who would lead people in exploring their parish boundaries need to plan the journey collaboratively. For clergy, that means paying attention to numbers even when we fear what they may imply—about our ministries and about ourselves. For lay leaders, that means taking the way of the Cross and embracing loss sometimes, especially when loss sows seeds of new life. (Sometimes just challenging habits can help people embrace a both/and perspective: My former senior warden, Stephen Rock, and I sometimes gave each other's reports, letting the tough management consultant talk about ministry and the kindly priest talk about numbers.) If we take that kind of collaborative approach, we can set aside the reporter/press secretary model at least long enough to allow new expressions of ministry, those fragile sparks of the Holy Spirit, to catch fire—or to burn out without judgment and recrimination. As Ian Mobsby notes, probably only one in five new expressions of ministry will survive (Mobsby). So as we beat our parish boundaries, congregational leaders would be well served to take the journey, and own the outcome, together.

Building the Kingdom or Putting Butts in Seats?

Several of the congregations I visited have struggled with an uncomfortable tension: In new expressions of ministry (and in inherited forms), are we striving to serve people around us and invite them to enter into the reign of God, or are we striving to build a religious organization and ensure its long-term well-being? Intellectually, we know the answer is a both/and, but the realities of church life pull us toward different sides of the equation in different moments.

At St. Paul's in Richmond, the Rev. Wallace Adams-Riley wrestles with the question personally and as a congregational leader. He says there's no simple answer to whether St. Paul's is putting resources into downtown mission out of an apostolic desire to share Good News or a desire to grow the organizational church. Simply wanting higher membership numbers seems crass, but expanding the assembly of Christ's disciples is what the Great Commission is all about—particularly when those disciples embrace their apostolic calling to go into the world in Christ's name. That ambivalence about motive "gets in the way of us simply saying, 'Yes! We want to grow our church, and that's one of our goals in downtown mission,'" Adams-Riley explained. "We still have not gotten as comfortable with that as I'd hoped" (Adams-Riley). But wherever its leaders' motives lie, St. Paul's has embraced the reality that success in downtown mission will not be quick. "We expected there would be slow growth," said Brian Levey, a vestry member, and they determined that success would be "establishing a regular pattern" of downtown ministry activities. "Eventually it would have a life of its own and develop a community" (Levey). Parish leadership bought into downtown mission for five years and committed to calling a downtown missioner. But even in that relatively nonanxious environment came expectations of measurable results. "After just a few months at St. Paul's, I was getting questions about when we would see more butts in the seats," said the Rev. Melanie Mullen, downtown missioner (Mullen). After a year and a half of Center gatherings, attendance has grown to about twenty—twice as many as when I visited.

In St. Mary's County, Maryland, three congregations creating new ministry together faced challenges not just in governance but in understanding success. The young lay leaders of Gather Eat Pray had a clear sense that their calling had little to do with butts in box pews. "Ultimately, we want more good people in the world," said Tom McCarthy, "and whether they end up being Episcopalian good people is immaterial" (McCarthy). But Phil Horne, treasurer of St. George's in Valley Lee, saw success differently: "The target of Gather Eat Pray is young adults who don't have any idea you ought to go to church. Hopefully, they catch the Good News and become better members of one of the parishes" (Horne). Other factors led directly to the demise of Gather Eat Pray, but that disconnect in defining success would have threatened it eventually.

Ministry thrives where leaders are on the same page. In Tewkesbury, England, everyone recognized that success for Celebrate! wouldn't happen quickly or inexpensively. The Rev. Wendy Ruffle explained that English pioneer ministers plan for *at least* one year of getting to know the community before offering anything that remotely resembles church ministry. Even past that point, when regular gatherings are taking place, "it's not about numbers," she said. "It's not about bums on seats. It's about who God wishes to draw here, who's hearing God's still, small voice" (Ruffle). The Rev. Paul Williams, abbey vicar, understood the timeline and the development process, so a lack of measurable results didn't fuel anxiety. They were also blessed with resources from an abbey trust, and later from the diocese, to support the ministry financially. "We knew we needed to be present first," he said. "Then that presence would properly turn into pastoring, and you can then turn to proclaiming, and then you can turn into being a prophet" by representing the community's interests to local leaders. "In each stage, you've got to build up trust as you go" (Williams).

Even with a successful new expression of ministry, growth may not show up as increases in attendance or membership on the annual report. At the Crossing in Boston, for example, the community gathers for worship on Thursday evening (thus not factoring into the cathedral's average Sunday attendance), and relatively few Crossing members officially join the cathedral. If a congregation offers something like Thirsty Theology or provides pastoral presence at a feeding program, the people it engages may well feel they have a spiritual community, and they might even be able to name the church that provides it. But whether that engagement grows into baptism, confirmation, or reception is a matter of long-term, one-on-one work. Even in the context of a worshiping community, long-term commitment happens less frequently now than generations ago. At St. Paul's in Seattle, lay pastor Paul Steinke says the congregation can't bank on worshipers at the 5 p.m. Community signing up for the long haul. About the young adults there, Steinke said, "We have them personally for a time. In their formation, this season—right now—is when I get to invest in them. It's this sort of rotating group of young adults who will invest for two or three years"—and then move on. Sometimes people choose to be connected but not on the sorts of terms churches find convenient. Steinke described one member of the 5 p.m. Community who has moved several times following a divorce in Seattle. "Now, we're Skyping with her," Steinke said. Church sometimes manifests itself as "a network of connection and community" rather than the *ecclesia* gathered in a certain place and time. "We're trying to help people not feel like, 'You've got to be *here, now*.'" But, at the same time, Steinke tries to thread the needle, forming the 5 p.m. Community to understand that community happens because people make the commitment to be present to it (Steinke).

Born with a Pledge Card in My Hand

Stephen Rock, my former senior warden, likes to say, "I was born with a pledge card in my hand." He comes from a long line of Episcopalians, and his parents impressed upon him both the social expectation and spiritual discipline of pledging to your parish. Unfortunately for the institutional church, there are fewer and fewer people like him as time goes on. And we struggle to know how to engage those who *weren't* born that way. Like the conflicted motivations that can lie behind evangelism, congregations struggle with how to preach stewardship without always seeming to be asking for money. Unless your congregation's endowment is huge, you know how the perceived scarcity of resources can hamper the best ideas. Of course, that holds true for new expressions of ministry, too. Money may not guarantee success, but scarce resources can almost certainly scuttle it.

For example, at St. Andrew and All Souls (SAAS) in Portland, the Rev. Karen Ward brings to her ministry the mind of a systematic theologian, expertise from founding Church of the Apostles in Seattle, and powerful leadership skills. What she doesn't have is money. The congregation is literally fifty to seventy-five people. Though she puts in full-time hours, her role is officially half-time (and she has indebted herself personally funding ministry costs). She wants to offer both an emergent-style mass and a standard Rite II Eucharist, but the budget won't allow twice the musical support. The missional initiatives she has in mind—renovating one building into a social services center and another into a café—will need outside grants to make them realities. "We have one problem right now, and that's money," Ward said. "Everything else— dealing with the old people and the young people—we've figured all that out" (Ward). So, despite the nearly miraculous success of SAAS's formation and weathering the storms of conflict, inadequate financial support threatens failure.

Though the need is now, Ward and SAAS are taking the long view, making giving part of its rule of life. Stewardship as a spiritual practice is part of the formation of all the new ministries I visited, with the exception of the Wilderness in Denver. There, the ministry's founders designed an experience that would erect no barriers, particularly for people who'd had a bad experience of church. For de-churched people in the cathedral's neighborhood, "we found they want a deeper relationship with the living God, and the reason they're giving up on the church is that the church has gotten in the way of that," explained the Rt. Rev. Peter Eaton, former dean (P. Eaton). For the Wilderness, part of the antidote from the start has been intentionally not asking worshipers for money or even raising the topic of stewardship. "We do not talk about it one iota," said the Rev. Jadon Hartsuff, who oversees the

Wilderness. "It's a dictum. We do not talk about stewardship in the Wilderness because the thought has been it will scare people away, and that's the last thing we want to do here" (Hartsuff). One may argue the benefits of that approach, but cathedral leaders, lay and ordained, have been consistent in standing by the principle—so the fact that the Wilderness will never pay for itself isn't perceived as a failure. The cathedral can, and does, cover the cost.

Other congregations I visited also have chosen to see the costs of missional expressions as the cost of doing the church's business. In Manchester, England, the Parish Church Council might grumble a bit about the expense of its several missional ministries, but "they're on board," said the Rev. Nick Bundock, rector. "We do wrestle with finance, but we don't point a finger at one particular cause of it" (Bundock). At St. Barnabas in London, the cost of ministry in the housing estate is seen in terms of following Jesus's path, giving oneself away for the sake of the gospel. "We're dealing with poverty there," said the Rev. Henry Kendal, vicar. "It's not realistic that Church@Five will ever be financially self-sustaining, and we have no expectation of it" (Kendal).

In Tewkesbury, leaders take the same perspective with Celebrate!, and they're considering how to take its countercultural success into the future. When Celebrate! was recognized as a worshiping community in its own right, that joy was tempered somewhat by the abbey's now-ongoing responsibility to support it. It's an example of the cost of ministry success: "The more it's worked, and the more it's become embedded in the ministry of the parish, the more we raise that question of sustainability," explained Graham Finch, former churchwarden at the abbey. "It becomes quite immediate and intense." But there seems to be a commitment to the ministry among the abbey's leadership, even if they're not sure yet precisely how it will be sustained. "We must continue it; it has transformed our ministry to the people on Prior's Park," Finch said. "And I'm sure there's much more transformational work to do. Building the kingdom is always work in progress, isn't it?" (Finch).

Lessons from the Field

Clearly, the most important part of defining success and failure in new expressions of ministry is actually to have the conversation among clergy and lay leaders. In Richmond, for example, the vestry and clergy developed a position description for a downtown missioner and committed to support the new ministry for five years. They left the specifics of downtown ministry largely to the Holy Spirit working through the clergyperson they would call, and they didn't get anxious when numbers hadn't increased in the first year. Mullen kept building relationships through community organizing and trying out different expressions of prayer and worship. And at this point, Center (just one example of St. Paul's downtown mission) gathers about twenty people a week.

Similarly, the senior clergy of the sponsoring congregation and those directly responsible for a new ministry need to be on the same page. Some of the congregations I visited revealed that alignment better than others. But in its own way, perhaps most noteworthy was St. James & Emmanuel in Manchester, England. There, the overall vision is the mustard tree that provides habitat for the birds of the air to nest (Mark 4:32). The congregation has a wide variety of people orbiting into and out of its worship and ministries—"people attending our church for all sorts of different reasons," as Bundock noted. "How do we infect that with an element of discipleship, an element of radicalization?" (Bundock). The Rev. Ben Edson, leader of the Abide community, also saw the need to form deeper identity, community, and discipleship at St. James & Emmanuel, and his experience was in forming new expressions of church as a pioneer minister. So Abide is an intentional community within the larger congregation "working within the institution toward being a renewal of the institution" (Edson). That degree of alignment helps both the inherited and new expressions of church there to assess progress and decide what to do next.

Once the leadership is in alignment, don't forget to build support for the new ministry within the congregation. If people don't understand new ministries, they're likely to regard them with suspicion and expect them to fail. Looking back on a very successful project in Boston, the Rev. Stephanie Spellers said she should have communicated with the cathedral more, and more intentionally, about the Crossing. Both the organizing model and the expression of its worship life were very different from what cathedral parishioners knew. "I should have been much more clear with the cathedral congregation about what worship, prayer, giving, and service would look like for the Crossing," she said (Spellers). Crossing members should have given regular updates during Sunday worship about how the new ministry was forming and what it was seeking to be and do, she explained. If people don't know about something, they can't see it succeed.

In assessing success or failure, the hardest part may be giving the ministry what will feel like an uncomfortably long time. With the exception of the Wilderness's invitational model, all the new ministries I visited are deeply relational undertakings, and relationships take time. Admittedly, that's relatively easy for the minister to say and harder for the treasurer to hear. But new expressions of ministry take patience, perseverance, and pastoral commitment probably more than anything else—as well as raising up leaders and sharing power, which is also time consuming. "There are no shortcuts," Spellers said. "You have to spend the time to build relationships, and you have to give up power as a clergyperson. Otherwise you'll end up with a service but not a community" (Spellers). Though leaders may be tempted to end new ministries, frustrated by the time it takes to see results, Edson actually argues the time it takes is a blessing. In a stand-alone fresh expression of church, "we could just go and do things; here, the process of change is much slower," Edson said. "But that can be a good thing, too, because the change is longer lasting and can carry more people with it. Change needs to rest with them and not with me" (Edson).

About financial challenges to new ministries' success, Mobsby has a single suggestion: Be entrepreneurial. Sitting in the one-third of St. Mary Aldermary that's a working café serving the financial district of central London, Mobsby pointed out that the institutional church—even in a nation where it receives state support—can't afford to fund ministries that take the church past its boundaries.

"In a post-Christian context, you can't rely on Big Cheese to give you the money, because the money's not there anymore," he said. And relying on volunteers and "tent makers" (people who lead ministry while holding secular jobs) is a recipe for burnout. "You have to be very entrepreneurial; we have to raise every single penny to do this," he said, looking around the café (Mobsby).

Probably the truest mark of success in new ministries, and the essential mark of sustainability, is investment by laypeople actually doing the work. In a small congregation, like SAAS, if the people don't pick up the torch, eventually the committed leader will burn out along with the missional fire. In a larger, more resourced congregation—particularly where the need for perceived success is strong—the temptation will arise to hire out the work. Depending on the ministry's scope, staff support may well be necessary. But as Adams-Riley notes, there's a difference between clergy or lay staff enabling the ministry of the baptized, and staff actually "doing the work for us." Garnering that lay involvement is essential— and, like the Trinity, one of the church's deepest mysteries. "What percentage of our people are actually willing to turn out on a Saturday, or sit in a coffee shop, in a spirit of downtown mission? That's where the rubber meets the road, and I'm not sure there's a harder bit of work than that," Adams-Riley said. "After all, most of the people in our congregation came to be part of the life of this church, not to be out in a mission context. That's not what brought them here" (Adams-Riley).

If It Doesn't Work, It May Not Be a Failure

Sometimes things simply won't work—even if the call was faithfully discerned, even if good planning built the ministry, even if people invested their hearts. And when things don't work, I find myself back at my desk as deputy press secretary more than twenty-five years ago, trying to explain why the governor's statement actually *wasn't* what he meant but just a thought in need of clarification. Maybe it *was* a mistake; but with a suspicious reporter on the phone, you don't use that word. Because if you do, you know it will be thrown back at you in the next news cycle.

So when parishioners come up to us and want to know if some ministry failed, we need to be able to say "yes" sometimes and explain why, rather than try to talk around it. If we're engaging the boundaries of our congregations and our hearts, we'll get the interactions wrong at least as often as we get them right—probably more often. Jesus didn't say, "Go and make disciples of all nations without making any mistakes." Perfectionism has no place in mission. As Mobsby said, "Read the Acts of the Apostles; I don't remember it not being messy" (Mobsby).

But sometimes, it is true that when things don't work, it's *not* a failure. Sometimes, what we get wrong isn't the ministry but the outcome we hope it will achieve. Author Nadia Bolz-Weber tells the story of Theology Pub, a bar conversation series she started early on in building the Church of All Sinners and Saints in Denver. She had hoped the gatherings would bring people into her new Sunday worshiping community—but they didn't. She began to see Theology Pub as a failure until she realized, "These events are an end—not a means to an end. We live out our life as a church in public, porous ways in which others are always invited to participate, and they do. The point is not to get them to join us on Sundays for the Eucharist. The point is that the Eucharist sustains us in the life we live out all week long, in which so many others participate" (Bolz-Weber 58).

That's not to say that I don't want to see more people coming to church on Sunday mornings. I do, and I hope ministries in my congregation will have that result. But it's not the only result that matters. I also want the church to see success when people come together in new ways, ministry that will never make it into the annual report.

References

Adams-Riley, Wallace. Personal interview by John Spicer. November 5, 2014.

Bolz-Weber, Nadia. "Operation: Turkey Sandwich." In *Ancient Faith, Future Mission: Fresh Expressions of Church and the Kingdom of God,* edited by Graham Cray, Aaron Kennedy, and Ian Mobsby, 51–58. Norwich, UK: Canterbury Press, 2012.

Bundock, Nick. Personal interview by John Spicer. October 24, 2014.

Eaton, Peter. Personal interview by John Spicer. September 20, 2014.

Edson, Ben. Personal interview by John Spicer. May 1, 2014.

Finch, Graham. Personal interview by John Spicer. October 12, 2014.

Hartsuff, Jadon. Personal interview 2 by John Spicer. September 21, 2014.

Horne, Phil. Personal interview by John Spicer. November 8, 2014.

Kendal, Henry. Personal interview 1 by John Spicer. July 8, 2014.

Levey, Brian. Personal interview by John Spicer. November 3, 2014.

McCarthy, Tom. Personal interview by John Spicer. November 10, 2014.

Mobsby, Ian. Personal interview by John Spicer. October 20, 2014.

Mullen, Melanie. Personal interview 1 by John Spicer. April 3, 2014.

Ruffle, Wendy. Personal interview 2 by John Spicer. October 10, 2014.

Simon, Paul. "Love and Hard Times." *So Beautiful or So What*, 2010. Available at: *http://www.paulsimon.com/track/love-and-hard-times/*. Accessed July 2, 2016.

Spellers, Stephanie. Personal interview by John Spicer. September 10, 2014.

Steinke, Paul. Personal interview 2 by John Spicer. October 5, 2014.

Ward, Karen. Personal interview 1 by John Spicer. July 10, 2014.

Williams, Paul. Personal interview 1 by John Spicer. July 17, 2014.

8

Beating the Bounds
with Every Step

> Then Jacob woke from his sleep and said, "Surely the LORD is in this place—and I did not know it!" And he was afraid, and said, "How awesome is this place! This is none other than the house of God, and this is the gate of heaven." —Genesis 28:16-17

AS THE ENGLISH MOVEMENT TOWARD mission-shaped church has recognized, being a missional congregation isn't about choosing the "right" strategy, despite how attractive particular ministries may be. Instead, a congregation lives missionally by asking two kinds of questions: What is the Good News for a particular community, and how is a particular congregation called to embody and proclaim it? (Bayes and Sledge 8–9).

But so often in church life—especially in our anxiety about survival and success—we're tempted to jump to answers first. I had lunch the other day with a parishioner who is critical of our congregation's redevelopment of our youth building as a resource for community members around us. He didn't oppose the intent of linking the parish with people on the boundaries of church life; he simply doubts that it will bring more people and more pledges into the congregation. Then he offered his right answer: "What you should do is look at the rock-n-roll churches and see how they're getting all those young people," he advised. There is truth in his suggestion; many of the "rock-n-roll churches" around us do a great job of welcoming people in, following up with them after a visit, listening to their spiritual needs, linking them with other church members and ministries, and explicitly connecting the congregation with the needs of the neighborhood, the city, and the world. But you don't have to have guitars and drums, hipster beards, and skinny jeans to follow those best practices. What you have to do is ask the right questions of the congregation and the context in which it finds itself.

The nine congregations I visited certainly asked those questions about missional DNA, whom to reach and how, discerning what God is trying to create, planning for leadership and governance, and assessing success or failure. But asking those questions may not necessarily lead to an answer that looks like offering alternative worship or opening a coffeehouse. Those questions may lead to answers the Church has known for centuries, in one form or another. As the Church of England's *Mission-Shaped Parish* argues, "Any expression of church can be shaped for mission, provided it takes its shape and its heart from what God has revealed and what the culture is saying" (Bayes and Sledge xi).

I hear that as good news because, as I said, I don't know whether a new expression of church will take root in my parish, no matter how much I think I'd like to see it. St. Andrew's in Kansas City may never raise up something like the Crossing or Celebrate! alongside our Sunday services. Is that OK? I think so—as long as what we *do* raise up "takes its shape and its heart from what God has revealed and what the culture is saying."

Remember those five questions that emerged as the congregations I studied developed their new expressions:

- Where's the mission in your DNA?
- Whom are you trying to reach—and how?
- What expression of ministry is God trying to create?
- How will you empower strong leadership and plan for governance?
- How will you identify success and failure?

What if those same questions guided all the ways ministry takes shape in our congregations, wherever those efforts fall on the spectrum of "inherited" to "fresh"? Those questions certainly apply to extreme forms of ministerial adaptation (new expressions), but they apply just as meaningfully to the choices we make about Sunday school, or serving hungry people, or inviting unchurched people into the congregation's life. They certainly apply to the choices we make in planning that good old Rite II liturgy, given Ian Mobsby's perspective that worship is more about empowering the present members of the Body of Christ for "contemplative action" to reach others rather than attracting unchurched people to a show that can't hope to compete with other forms of popular entertainment (Mobsby). Think of the benefit we might see if we applied the rigor of those five questions to our discernment about ministries we've come to regard as "what we've always done."

That's happening in some of the congregations I visited. Think about St. Andrew and All Souls (SAAS) in Portland. There, the Rev. Karen Ward began by creating an emergent worship experience alongside an existing inherited form. And she hopes to return to that both/and approach, accommodating different worshiping communities within the same parish. But for Ward, reaching the parish—in a larger, geographic sense—is the point, and every aspect of SAAS's life intends to connect the congregation with its community. Some elements align with new church expressions (innovative musical styles, shared preaching, neomonasticism, social enterprise, radical welcome, etc.), and some are ministries that have been in the Anglican wheelhouse for centuries (connecting the arts and spirituality, praying the Daily Office, feeding the poor, getting involved in local civic life, opening the church building to the community). In every ministry, SAAS has mission first in mind. "My vision for the place is an ethos about Eucharist—feeding people, offering hospitality," Ward said. "That's our paradigm, and it has to go through all the ministries we're doing" (Ward).

Think about St. James & Emanuel in Manchester, England. Its new expression of church, Abide, is described as the congregation's "missional community," and it's featured among the examples of fresh expressions on the Church of England's website (Edson). But St. James & Emmanuel incarnates mission to its community across its programs and ministries, particularly through offering its facilities as points of connection with its neighbors. Renting out its parish center, providing space for a social-enterprise youth café, or housing refugees may or may not qualify as new expressions of church. But in them—as in its varied worship styles and its partnership with two schools—St. James & Emmanuel has found ways to go to people on the boundaries of English post-Christian culture. Everything St. James & Emmanuel does extends the branches of the kingdom's mustard tree, inviting local birds of the air to come and nest.

In my congregation, as we redevelop our old youth building into a center for the parish and community, we're using this kairotic moment to learn to see traditional categories of ministry in newly missional terms. Perhaps the best example is "formation" (a word I find parishioners chafe against because it sounds too much like church-speak). Those of us of a certain age will remember when this set of ministries was "Christian education"; and at least at Christ Church in Springfield, Missouri, where I grew up, it consisted of Sunday school, youth group, and the rector's forum on Sunday mornings, complete with what seemed like hundreds of dirty ashtrays on the tables in the parish hall. Like the citizens of Lake Wobegon, all our Christian education programs were strong, good-looking, and above average—at least in historical memory. And they were definitely educational, transmitting the orthodoxy of Episcopal Christianity to people in a "believe, become, and (hope to) belong" model of church. Just ask any of us who literally memorized the catechism in order to graduate from confirmation class.

Over the past few years, St. Andrew's, like many congregations, has been trying to change its formational model in terms of content, structure, and leadership. The Sunday "rector's forum" has been replaced by a variety of groups and learning opportunities led by laypeople and lay staff—and involving more participants. We've begun a catechesis process for adults, moving from a short "Episcopal 101" to an inquirers' class on the sacraments to an exploration of the Baptismal Covenant in preparation for baptism, confirmation, reception, or reaffirmation. Children's formation is also shifting away from exclusively Sunday morning classes, now including more special events and tools to help parents form their children's faith at home. Youth formation remains the greatest challenge because of kids' (and parents') involvement beyond church, as well as our too-long reliance on the model of weekly youth group. But we're trying to leverage strong acolyte and Scout programs into opportunities for deeper faith formation and more service in the community.

Now, as part of beating our boundaries in our congregation's neighborhood, we're trying to make formation a more explicit point of connection with people around us. Remembering Mobsby's progression of orthopathy, orthopraxis, and orthodoxy in forming Christian community—and listening to the people around us—we're seeking to become a better resource for personal and community well-being, which is certainly a component of building relationships and building the kingdom. Talking with people in our neighborhood, we heard a desire for a place for kids to play and have team practices, a place for parties and receptions, and resources to build parenting and relationship skills. At the same time, we've identified a calling to create an incubator for social entrepreneurial start-ups and to gather people to explore the intersection of spirituality and the arts. Add to this our concurrent need to steward a dilapidated youth building, and we found a missional initiative we call Gather & Grow. But this is no slam dunk. I don't have a script to follow. We're seeking to build new ministries and take existing ministries in new directions, and change is not any congregation's strong suit. But trying to imagine ministries like formation in newly missional terms seems like the right road ahead, especially as it intersects with needs expressed in the community.

No doubt, the specifics of St. Andrew's call will change with time and as we learn better to listen to the people at the edges of our self-imposed boundaries. But stepping out seems a holy orientation. Mobsby compares the church's present moment, as we move from Christendom into whatever comes next, with the historical context of monasteries at the time of the Reformation.

They had become "places of private prayer where the monks had privilege and were withdrawn from the world," he said, and the church struggled with how to make the monasteries resources to the geographic parishes around them. Now, parish churches struggle with the same call to become greater resources to the communities in which they're located. "I think this is what parishes are called to be," Mobsby said, in relation to the de-churched and the unchurched. "I don't think we would have a crisis in mission if the parish understood itself as a missional community. It changes everything if we exist for who's *not* here, rather than existing for ourselves" (Mobsby).

References

Bayes, Paul, and Tim Sledge. *Mission-Shaped Parish: Traditional Church in a Changing World*. New York: Seabury, 2010.

Edson, Ben. "Abide." Last modified October 22, 2012. Accessed November 15, 2015. *https://www.freshexpressions.org.uk/stories/abide*.

Mobsby, Ian. Personal interview by John Spicer. October 20, 2014.

Ward, Karen. Personal interview 1 by John Spicer. July 10, 2014.

9

People Are the New Program

"The Word became flesh and blood, and moved into the neighborhood." —John 1:14 (*The Message*)

IN 2013, BEFORE MY SABBATICAL PROJECT was much more than a twinkle in my eye, I made a pilgrimage to Thad's in Santa Monica, California. Thad's is a "mission station" of the Episcopal Diocese of Los Angeles, an experimental church community finely tuned to the context it serves. It meets in commercial space rather than a churchy-looking building; it offers music that fits the hip Santa Monica scene; its sermons are dialogical and track with people's real-life concerns. Thad's is church for people "who would never otherwise darken the door of one of our traditional parishes," as its founder, the Rev. Jimmy Bartz, puts it ("Laundry Love Venice Beach"). Walking in, you might not even realize it *is* a church, much less an Episcopal congregation. But worshiping there, you feel the place tingle with incarnation. Sounds like Anglicanism to me.

Thad's intrigued me because Bartz did such a great job of "double listening," that work underlying fresh expressions in England—listening to both the context around him and the witness of Scripture and tradition. I had no intent to replicate Thad's in my congregation; but I put photos from my visit in the bulletin the next Sunday, preached about exploring the context around us, and probably scared a lot of people.

On Thad's website (*http://thads.church*), you find videos that profile the congregation, discuss surfing as a spiritual practice, and document a ministry there called Laundry Love. It's something other churches are doing, too (including St. Paul's in Richmond as part of its downtown mission): Parishioners go to a local laundry and do wash for people in need. It's both a stunning witness of love and powerful formation in servant ministry.

But watching the Laundry Love video, what struck me even more than the modern-day footwashing was Bartz's distillation of the principle that underlies all of Thad's ministry. As Bartz puts it, "People are the new program" ("Laundry Love Venice Beach"). Someone else may have said it first, but Bartz captured what I've found to be the common strand woven through all the new expressions of ministry I visited. From Seattle to London, people are the new program.

For a cradle Episcopalian like me, it's a simple but seismic shift in thinking about how congregations might seek both to reveal the kingdom of God and steward the institutional church. We've spent a lot of time, and set a lot of congregational DNA, developing programs. It's the attractional model of American Christianity, which combines the mindset of Christendom ("good people go to church") with the mindset of consumerism ("people choose products and experiences that best meet their needs") to produce a variety of options designed to attract those good people to our pews. If our programs are good, the logic goes, we'll get a strong enough market share to keep the institution growing. Thad's, along with the congregations I visited, is coming at the challenge from the bottom up—not "What can the church offer that might bring people in?" but "What are people wanting, and needing, and already doing in the communities our churches serve?"

It's vital to note that what many people want and need is inherited church. Much is wonderful, and healthy, and life-giving about inherited church. I'm a Rite II kind of guy; the reason I studied the congregations I chose was because they were honoring and practicing inherited church while they raised up new ministries alongside or within it. For inherited church, the reorientation that comes with "people are the new program" is this: We would offer Rite I and Rite II services on Sunday morning not because we've always done it that way, or because the prayer book says to, but because there are real, live human beings who would build relationships with Jesus Christ through that worship.

And there are. As we beat the boundaries of our parishes, we will find them. In my own context, we find the classic "instant Episcopalians"—couples coming from Roman Catholic and Protestant backgrounds looking for a married middle way. We find de-churched Roman Catholics who miss not just the seven Sacraments but the sacramental universe and who discover a welcoming home with us they'd never imagined. We find de-churched Protestants like the young woman I met in Seattle, spiritually exhausted from being asked to gin up charismatic fervor every Sunday and longing to explore the mystery of God's Word at something deeper than its surface level. We find unchurched Nones who'd imagined Christianity meant institutions protecting their own interests by excluding voices from the margins, telling people what to believe, and asking them for money—but who then encounter a broken, real gathering of God's people loving them for who they are.

And as we beat those boundaries, we'll also find people who aren't looking to come into the church per se but who *are* looking for relationship with God and other pilgrims—which, by the way, is who we are, especially as we journey to the edges of our institutional worlds. We'll find people, like the young adults in downtown Boston, who want to "love people hard, give power away, and orient ourselves toward God," as one member put it (Mills-Curran). We'll find people, like the Goths and legislative staffers in Denver, who want a safe place to encounter deep mystery. We'll find people, like the hipsters in Portland and the former evangelicals in Seattle, who want to know a God who takes embodied life seriously. We'll find people, like the residents of Prior's Park in Tewkesbury and Strawberry Vale in London, who've heard the culture say their lives don't matter and who want good news from a higher authority instead. We'll find people, like the everyday folks in Manchester, who want a community and a God to whom they can commit their whole hearts. We'll find people, like the loft-dwellers and bureaucrats in Richmond, who want shelter from the storm and a witness that God dwells with them. We'll find people, like the young adults in southern Maryland and the stewards of their congregations, who want church to speak with new words and dance with new steps.

Whether they're looking for church as we've known it or looking for a God beyond knowing, those real people must be our focus. We won't be the right community for all of them, probably not even for most of them. We'll find that, in their orbits of spiritual seeking, they might be with us for a season—perhaps months, perhaps years, perhaps decades. We can't offer something to meet everyone's needs, but we can offer ourselves, our souls and bodies and the DNA we bear: a flesh-and-bones approach to worship and spiritual practice, an inclusive approach to theology, a collaborative approach to governance, and a big-tent approach to honoring one another in polarized times.

In Christ, God chose to invest in real people. "The Word became flesh and blood and moved into the neighborhood," as John's Gospel tells us (1:14, The Message). When we beat the boundaries of our own neighborhoods, we'll find real people, just as Jesus did. We can continue to offer them what we've always served up, or we can follow Jesus's path. He didn't speak to everyone the same way. He didn't tell the same parable over and over again. And he urges us, too, to dig deeply into the treasure of Scripture, tradition, and reason—and into the treasure of our own loving hearts—to offer people what they need, not just what we're used to giving. Jesus asks each congregation, the family of God neighborhood by neighborhood, to be like the "master of a household who brings out of his treasure what is new and what is old" (Matt. 13:52).

I take comfort in that. There is room in this mixed economy of God's church for Laundry Love and Jewell Room receptions, for community organizers and women's guild presidents, for worship in the Wilderness and a good old Rite II. By the same token, there is need in this extended family of God's church for each one of us who's been commissioned in baptism and sent out along the Way. I'm no church guru, but I can walk alongside people, listen to them, tell the stories of the journey, and mark signposts for the next pilgrim. On that journey, we each have gifts to offer—and we each have to offer them. No one can cross our boundaries for us.

But together, we can go all the way out to the creek or the fence that has enclosed our pleasant land, extend a hand to the person we see there, and begin a conversation about what it's like to be on the other side.

References

"Laundry Love Venice Beach." Accessed January 28, 2016. *http://thads. church/videos/*.

Mills-Curran, Mary Beth. Personal interview by John Spicer. September 4, 2014.